ADD A Z€RO

Brian O'Connor has been the *Irish Times* racing correspondent since 1997. He lives in County Wicklow with his wife and two children.

ADD A Z€RO

Brian O'Connor

HACHETTE
BOOKS
IRELAND

First published in 2008 by Hachette Books Ireland

Copyright ©, Brian O'Connor, 2008

1

The right of Brian O'Connor to be identified as the Author of the Work has been asserted by him in accordance with the Copyright, Designs and Patents Act, 1988.

A CIP catalogue record for this title is available from the British Library.

ISBN: 978-0-340-9607-38

Typeset in Adobe Garamond and Univers by Hachette Books Ireland
Cover and text design by Anú Design, Tara
Printed and bound in Great Britain by Mackays of Chatham Ltd, Chatham, Kent

Hachette Books Ireland's policy is to use papers that are natural, renewable and recyclable products and made from wood grown in sustainable forests. The logging and manufacturing processes are expected to conform to the environmental regulations of the country of origin.

Hachette Books Ireland
8 Castlecourt Centre, Castleknock, Dublin 15, Ireland

A division of Hachette Livre, 338 Euston Road, London NW1 3BH, England

Contents

Preface ix

1 Sammy the Snake and the 'Big L' 1

2 And God Created Paradise 12

3 Will Perv for Money 24

4 Me and Warren Beatty .36

5 My Vibrating Virgil 46

6 Nuking Dougie 56

7 Frankie's Deep-Throat Potion 66

8 SpongeBob's Ulster Fry 78

9 The Fallon Idol 85

10 Triers to the Front! 95

11 The Tall Thin Buddha .103

12 Power Sharing Doesn't Work 117

13   Eddie G.'s Cool Too 131

14   Saigon Crypto and the Stiff Upper Lip 139

15   Bertie's Black Beauty Boob 148

16   A Peep at the Future 158

17   Irish Bird is Mad! 168

18   The Price of Ignoring Rita 178

19   Genius Doesn't Need Money 191

20   The St Bernard Casino 202

21   Billy Hogarth's Slow Progress 213

22   Everyone's Favourite Day-Release Programme . .220

23   It's Fate – With a Plan! 227

24   Beached on the Nile 233

25   Just Think Gandhi 242

26   Aw, Crap 248

Acknowledgements 250

To Niamh and the boys

Preface

Books like this usually navigate a thin line between advice and entertainment, so those of you looking for a 'how to' manual should walk away now. Never mind the obvious evidence that such efforts are mostly churned out by those whose advice should only be sought on how to fleece the gullible; it's also dangerous to expect expertise on anything where over-whelming evidence to the contrary is provided daily. As a racing correspondent on a national newspaper, the obvious deduction to be gained from providing tips on the horses is that if they were any good, I wouldn't have to provide them in the first place. It is J.P. McManus, and not yours truly, who is sitting in his own hotel in Barbados, having individually peeled grapes dropped into his expensively dentined maw by platoons of dusky locals so beautiful they make the wondrous Merlene Ottey look like she's let herself go. Or at least, that's what I dream is happening. One thing I am willing to bet on, however, is that racing's most famous gambler was in school the last time he found himself dispensing tips, and primary school at that.

As for any entertainment quotient, the quips that dipped and swooped like swallows in a heat wave when this idea was being pitched to the publisher, sound a hell of a lot more glacial now that they face the arctic vastness of the blank page. Einstein joked that the secret of creativity is to know how to hide your sources: mine are so well hidden that I've forgotten where to start looking.

Instead, it has become increasingly obvious that the under-lying pulse of this book is confessional. Sure enough, where there is a confession to be told, there is also a good measure of guilt to be heaved overboard. And where there's guilt, there is usually a crime. I don't believe that making a living from tipping horses is a criminal offence – although there have been occasions when disgruntled punters have advised that a cell would be too good for me. Indeed, on one memorable occasion during Listowel race week, a saintly looking old lady transformed into a wrinkly Boadicea when informed of who she was talking to, and loudly proclaimed that I couldn't tip shit out of a bucket.

But absolving oneself of a criminal impulse is no sop to a guilty conscience. Making a living from your hobby is a privilege accorded to a very tiny minority. The least those of us who have selfishly squeezed fate's lucky glands dry can do is to take our good fortune seriously. And yet, for some time, there has been no getting away from the gnawing realisation that that particular side of the bargain is being let down.

Not in any professional way. Covering the horses, like any other form of journalism, demands the appropriate number of words being delivered on time to the correct place. To say there is a skill needed to do this is to fairly baste oneself in buttery self-regard. It's more a temperament thing, or maybe at best, a craft. But it is also blindingly obvious we are not talking about Heisenberg's breakthrough in matrix mechanics here.

All of which is not to say that just anyone can do it. The world is full of millions of sporting fanatics who have sub-limated so much useless information that they can tell you who played right-back on the Andorran soccer team that played Upper Volta in the 1962 Who Gives A Crap Cup. In com-parison, racing inhabits its own peculiar little cosmos where fans are pulled remorselessly towards its throbbing heartbeat, while those who hate it would rather be banished to the farthest extremities of non-gravitational hell. There is no middle ground with the gee-gees. It's either love or hate, with no com-fortable refuge for the crucial remote-control punching, floating viewer.

That is good news for those of us sufficiently familiar with the language and mores of the game to at least give the impression of competence. If, in addition, you are capable of stringing some sentences together, then a sort of journalistic nirvana is achieved, whereby the hack is largely left alone and the boys back in editorial base can concentrate on what really matters, like Wayne Rooney's big toe.

However, familiarity is able to smuggle, if not contempt,

then at least a deep and comfortable rut into any heaven. And often the only way out is with a defiant gesture.

Sir Peter O'Sullevan, the legendary BBC commentator, believes passionately that every racing journalist has to bet. There is no other way to engage with the reader, he believes. If the hack can't be bothered to back his opinion, then why should punters? O'Sullevan, who in the 1950s formed a legendary partnership with Clive Graham in the *Daily Express*, also likes to pose a question to his colleagues. 'Given the choice, what would you rather: tip a big-priced winner of a big race or break a great story?'

O'Sullevan always says the tip is the thing. I would go for the story every time. Maybe that's training or inclination – or both. But it's increasingly feeling like a copout. Professional detachment is one thing: deliberate distance is another. Sure, I like a flutter but I can't remember the last time it mattered enough to get my palms sweaty. There is also the rather obvious dilemma of putting so-called expertise out there to the general public and then not being prepared to back it up with cash. What kind of 'expert' doesn't follow his own advice?

It's time to at least try and do that with my €5,000 and maybe even make it pay. After all, there are betting beasts out there who manage to make money out of their gambling, although they are increasingly being captured for conservation purposes.

The cliché about never meeting a poor bookie has burrowed its way into the public consciousness like a prurient tick, but that doesn't mean it is enshrined in some gambling law that our horse-loving politicians have slipped through parliament. John McCririck, for instance, is a former bookie who couldn't make it pay. So there must at least be some chance of turning a profit from betting, and a chance is all anyone can ask for.

It's not as if I haven't had times in the past when my eye and luck and whatever punting fates there are in the sky, had merged for long enough to come off in a big way. There was that silly little £5 double on the Irish Guineas a few years ago: the horses were 33–1 and 20–1 and it paid up over £3,500. Or when Dermot Weld gave the nod on the morning of the 1993 Melbourne Cup that Vintage Crop was on the verge of history and those Aussie bookies were so generous with their 20–1.

It isn't like I'm starting from scratch. I know people in the game. I hear information many punters would kill for. Why can't it pay off?

The flat season is just about to start, running from March to early November. The timing is ideal. At the very least, it means not having to cope with valuable investments falling on their arses at the last fence. During the summer, there is racing every day in Ireland and an absolute deluge available from around the world to fill in any gap, more than enough material to see if it's possible to make betting the horses come up aces.

As for the basic idea for this project, I want to acknowledge two young schoolboys I overheard on the Luas one day doing their maths homework. One kept saying to his pal – 'Just add a zero. How hard can that be?'

It would be nice to say they ignited a little passion in a middle-aged man but, since that would be to risk a visit from the police and a platoon of tabloid reporters, let's just leave it at thanks.

Brian O'Connor
February 2007

Sammy the Snake
and the 'Big L'

25 March

A strange yellow object hovers over the Curragh. At times, it even produces some heat, which prevents the rest of us dismissing the sun-worshippers as heretics and torching their pagan carcasses over a spit to create some warmth. It is all remarkably pleasant, which has the more sceptical checking their diaries.

The opening day of the flat is not supposed to be like this. Usually, Irish racing's headquarters greets the 'summer game' with the sort of weather that normally parks down at the Falkland Islands and makes a once-a-year vacation north just to remind itself of how wonderful the scenery is back home. Ireland is a cold spot in March anyway, but nowhere can seem more miserable than the flat plain of the Curragh. When those northerlies blow, only a few thousand morose sheep relentlessly tearing at Kildare's bald, green pate are reckless enough to venture out: the sheep, and a few thousand race-goers determined to welcome in racing's very own changing of the seasons.

It's only nine days since Cheltenham, the pinnacle of the winter game, finished up. In a couple of weeks' time, the English and Irish Grand Nationals will be run and Punchestown is waiting at the end of April. Sandwiched in between all these determinedly raucous dates is today: flat racing's first faltering steps to try and re-establish its more cerebral hold over the public imagination. Come the Derby in June, it will have done so, but on Day One, having to switch focus can feel like a duty, like when you are a kid at a wedding and despatched to look after the younger cousins.

Except it is different today, the start of the most noble experiment since Newton wondered why he liked the colour red so much – or something like it anyway. Lying ahead are seven months when it will be established if €5,000 can be turned into €50,000 – adding a zero.

Ignoring the cries of a wife and two children, as any good scientist would, the fund – or 'tank' as it is known in betting circles – has been created by also ignoring the creaking demands of an eight-year-old car to receive the scrapyard's final merciful bullet. All it has to do is keep going for another little while, then we'll be able to afford it a wonderful retirement in its own little paddock where it can happily rust into oblivion. As for the kids, their own shots will also just have to wait. Nothing can dampen this optimism. It surely can't be a coincidence that the sun is shining. This is fate, a sunny start to a bright future.

Some familiar faces start to appear. Michael Kinane walks quietly by and makes for the ancient jockeys-room that has been his office and spiritual home for over thirty years. Like most of the top riders, he has spent much of the winter in Dubai, fighting the never-ending battle against his own body weight. He looks well on it, though. Tanned and fit. That famously tough forty-seven-year-old face, perched on top of a schoolboy body, is even relaxed enough to offer some quiet greetings. Back again for another season – how enthusiastic is that?

Kinane isn't alone. Crushing disappointment may be only one race away but, right now, anything is possible. For the owner, that six-figure purchase who steadfastly refuses to approach a decent speed on the home gallops might just be saving his best for the track, an equine Socrates able to ponder the philosophical percentages of when to sweat and when to just simply chill. There isn't a trainer alive willing to give up the ghost as long as there is at least one well-bred two-year-old that hasn't galloped and revealed his talent yet. And as for jockeys, well, they're a separate breed again, blessed by nature with the lack of stature needed for their unique occupation and cursed by the scales to a carbohydrate-free existence of fresh air and little else.

It's been almost five months since a flat race has been run in Ireland. Some of the horses have run over hurdles during the winter but most haven't, and so the usual tortuous attempts to link and compare form lines are redundant. One horse might be clearly superior to the opposition on last year's form but, if he has eaten like a hungry grizzly during the winter, he might not be able to get his legs around his gut. The result is that everyone is going around the place, trying to find out which horses are ready to run for their lives and which of them couldn't run for a bus. It is particularly true of those beasties that are having their first ever racecourse starts. They are the real dreamboats, never mind that most of them will end up breathlessly chasing mere adequacy. For the moment, they are all Nijinsky incarnate – and one in particular might just be. That's why I'm already displaying the sort of smug satisfaction Sylvester the Cat will have if he ever does finally tuck into Tweety Bird.

The word on this miracle of equine design didn't come from just anywhere. This was no second-hand whisper from a wiry drunk in a Kildare pub. In fact, as tips go, it was snobbish enough to have been conceived and hatched by the Mrs Chairman of every rugby club in Cork city.

The Moyglare Dinner is an annual pre-Christmas bash at the K-Club where the great and the good accumulate to pat racing on the back and reassure it of its rightful place at the centre of the universe. Some of the racing media are brought along too, in the same way that brown bread is used for a little roughage with some of the very luxurious pâté. Normally, it is a rather worthy and dull exercise but last time was different. The table draw put Kevin Prendergast in the next-door stall and, in the process, changed an otherwise predictable evening into a mini-tutorial in the ways of the horse.

Prendergast is seventy-four, looks twenty years younger and

has the sort of brio usually found only in Frenchmen living next to a brothel. Training racehorses has been his life, it's been bred into him and is still a source of fascination. That much is obvious in the way he tells a yarn; and he has plenty of those, most of them libellous but all the funnier for their flamboyant lack of propriety. There is a tolerance there too, and even his audience's guffaws and increasingly bleary eyed demands for more didn't send him sprinting for the cloakroom.

Towards the end, however, he leant conspiratorially across and, *sotto voce*, advised about a filly so talented she deserved the ultimate accolade from a professional horseman – 'This is a fucking machine.' That was enough to prompt me to come up for a breath of sober air.

'What's her name?'

'Reggie something,' he said. 'But she's out of Rebelline. Belongs to the O'Reillys. She's had a few little problems. We couldn't run her at two. But they won't see which way she goes when we do get her out. Just you wait.'

And there was a delay, of sorts, until getting home when a full-scale search of every racing website and publication revealed that Rebelline's daughter is called Regalline. Already the picture of her sprinting clear on her first start to win at 10–1 was forming. Kevin would welcome her back to the winner's enclosure and slyly wink over at the chortling hack busy trousering a five-figure sum just as Sir Tony, Mr Bean himself, arrives in, demanding why nobody had told him to back it. Through a cold winter, the idea was enough to warm more than a few cockles. Now that the day had finally come, there were enough cockles roasting to send any concept of doubt shrivelling into oblivion.

Regalline is due to run in the second race, the six-furlong maiden. Twenty-five three-year-olds are lining up. Twelve of them have never run before. Regalline might not end up at 10–1 but there should still be some kind of decent price around. It is in such exploratory form that I make my visit to bookmaker's ring in front of the stands just as the runners for the first race begin to canter past to the start.

Racecourse bookies are a curious breed, but no longer in the sense of the clichéd popular perception. In Britain, it is almost a breach of the Trade Descriptions Act if bookmakers aren't either roguish Terry-Thomas-type hustlers or homicidal maniacs who'll be after your thumbs with a pliers if you don't cough up. There are a few in the ring in Ireland who are playing out their lives in a movie in their heads – all pin-striped suits and slicked-back hair, bling jangling on their wrists – but most could be businessmen in the city if you met them away from the racecourse. It's not surprising either. This year, almost €200 million will be handled by on-course book-makers. They might sometimes have to stand on boxes in weather you wouldn't put a dog out in but, for that kind of money, most of us would put our mothers out into a hurricane.

Anyway, these days, instead of chalk and a loaded syringe, no bookie can turn up for work without a laptop. The impact of internet betting exchanges has been so immense that venturing into the cauldron of the betting ring without one is to invite a quick and expensive commercial death. No one has to hide behind bushes to watch morning workouts any more. Today, all a racecourse bookmaker has to do is switch on a computer and watch what's hot and what's not. It's a comfortable state of affairs compared to just a few years ago when the appearance of a heavy hitter in the ring could have the same effect as a fox in a hen-house. It still happens, except now the hens have radar.

At the Curragh, the top of the betting ring begins almost exactly at the finish line, so it is easy to see how the bookmakers are betting on the opening race as sixteen two-year-olds, all racing for the first time, canter past. Every second one of them shies at the same spot, eyeing the large red finishing post suspiciously and forcing their riders to crouch low and encourage them forward with a tap of the whip down the shoulder. Even at two years of age and at half-speed, there's a power and a fluidity to the horses that make the jockeys' skill in successfully remaining perched on top of them impressive. The point is emphasised even more when one of the horses flashes past unencumbered by a little man on his back. A quick peep over the rails reveals a mercifully unhurt jockey, David Moran, hopefully running after his mount. He's carrying the colours of the number seven horse, Sammy The Snake, who is galloping in the general direction of Kildare town. Genetically, Moran has the size requirements for his profession but those same genes haven't really equipped him with the stride to catch up with his partner. Still, at least there's one runner to discount.

There have been persistent tips for at least five of the others who represent most of the top yards in the country. But the most persistent of all has been for Dermot Weld's Jade Mountain. A cursory look in the paddock has resulted in the conclusion that the colt has four legs and is able to walk in a straight line. Apart from that, he looks no more exceptional than any of the others. However, the chat in the weigh room is that DK, as Dermot Kenneth Weld is generally known, thinks he's going to have a good day. It's enough. How appropriate to have the first bet of the new season on the first race.

The betting is wide open. Aidan O'Brien could run a cross-eyed jennet in a two-year-old race and it would start favourite, but a €300,000 colt rejoicing under the name of Georgebernardshaw is weaker in the market than the old fraud's handshake. He drifts right out to 5–1. Jade Mountain slides too, out to 4–1 and yet there's no huge support for anything else. A quick glance at the big screen in front of the stands: they're starting to load up. Ciaran Skelly, one of the bigger bookmakers in the ring, presses a button and the price on Jade Mountain flashes 9–2 in digital red. Another look at the screen: there's only a few to go. What the hell, let's start as we mean to go on. Skelly takes my €50 and swaps it for a ticket quicker than Colin Farrell can drop trou'.

The race is over the minimum distance of five furlongs and, even allowing for the testing ground conditions, it takes less than seventy seconds. Standing at ground level on the line and watching on the big screen, it is immediately obvious that Jade Mountain is well prepared. Whereas some of the others are being pushed from the start, this little colt with the big white noseband travels easily: a bit farther back than ideal, but going well enough to make up ground – except he doesn't. When the horses rumble close enough to make the screen unnecessary, he resolutely remains in fifth as a horse with light-blue colours flashes past just ahead of a horse carrying yellow. The winner's saddle cloth has the number seven on it. Sammy The *bloody* Snake has won.

When they get loose like that, the jockey is supposed to be eventually reunited with the horse before lobbing gently back to protect the damn thing for the next day. What is not supposed to happen is that they run loose over a large area and then still have enough puff left to win.

In the winner's enclosure, his trainer looks like he's about to spontaneously combust with happiness. Brendan Duke is an Irishman based in England. The fact that he has come all the way home to run the horse must have tipped off some people. But still.

It's only fifty quid but it is not a good start, and good starts are important. The concept of luck might be abstract in theory but even just a nodding acquaintance with betting the horses tells you the 'Big L' hangs over every punter. If you don't begin well, it means your eye isn't in and, before you know it, you're circling the drain to financial disaster.

Still, there's Regalline to come next. Kevin Prendergast hasn't got to where he is by depending on luck. Instead, he has the twinkle-eyed shrewdness of a man who hasn't taken a stupid breath in decades. He'd even told us about his last stupid act: driving in northern Queensland in the 1950s in a heat wave when the car broke down – 'It was a twenty mile walk to the nearest town: thought I was fucked.'

The opening show in the ring for the six furlong maiden has Regalline a clear 7–4 favourite. Kevin must have talked a hell of a lot more since Christmas and really got into gear during Lent. There are pigeons roosting in the eaves of the old stand who know about Regalline, and they haven't even been caught by her during some of these spectacular morning workouts. Amongst the bookies, she's already old news before she has even run – like an *X-Factor* winner with a first record that people can't be bothered to buy.

No matter if this filly is running on jet-fuel, this is a ridiculous price. She has never run. The experience of coming to the races, parading in front of people and then having to run against twenty-four others might melt her mind. It happens. Poor house registers through the centuries are full of the names of dumb saps who have punted their brains out on morning glories. Regalline was a bet to dream of at a reasonable price, but not now.

Still, she is supposed to be some sort of world beater. Imagine if she wins the Guineas back here in May? How stupid will it be to have to tell someone about knowing the inside track on the great Regalline six months before she even ran and not backing her in a maiden because she was a bad price? This could be one of those any-price-is-a-good-price moments. The runners are at the post. It will take some time to lead them up. Maybe someone will go twos.

Not only does 2–1 come along, but Regalline slips out to 5–2, by which time, all this internal debate has concluded that she has to be backed. It's just €50, enough to get the €50 back from the first with some change. Nothing serious. Having waited for her since before Christmas, how sick would I feel if she wins unbacked? That really would be fate. The gates open just as the ticket changes hands.

Regalline finishes second: she has every chance. There's no point labelling the jockey a cretinous idiot who has just destroyed a winter of contented anticipation. If the horse is really as good as all the talk, then she would have won. The real toppers don't have to have excuses made for them.

Another filly having her first start, a 20–1 shot called Once Upon A Grace wins. Afterwards, her trainer, Frances Crowley, talks about going for a classic trial next. Says she has always thought a lot of Once Upon A Grace. The starting price, however, indicates that she kept that regard mostly to herself. Maybe that's the best way, although it doesn't seem as much fun.

A hundred quid down might be nothing, but it's still annoying. What were the reasons for betting on two horses that had never run before? Jade Mountain was because of a silly sentimental idea that the first race should be marked by something – like marking it with €50 more in my pocket than there is now wouldn't have been enough of a statement. As for Regalline, every instinct had been screaming to get my sorry ass out of the betting ring and, when it comes to the horses, switching from your gut instinct is fatal.

Besides, betting seriously when the ground is more suitable to mud-loving Grand National winners than daisy-cutting Derby contenders is a futile exercise: the worst kind of mug punting. It's time to pull the oars in for a while and wait until they might not be needed on some of the racetracks. Now is the time to build some foundations, and tomorrow morning will be the perfect start.

Running total: - €100

And God Created Paradise

26 March

Peter O'Shea was faster than me, much better at football too, and he knew way more about Vincent O'Brien's horses. His granny used to live next door to us and, every so often, Peter's mum would drive down from the city to visit her and he would be released to hang out with the neighbour. We used to swap shoes and old copies of the *Irish Racing Annual* in which O'Brien, the greatest horse trainer of them all, gave little one-line nuggets about some of the horses he thought might be good. Sitting on the footpath, we pored over them like archaeologists on a dig. We were eight. Even then, it was impossible not to be impressed when Peter came up with the name of Gregorian and said he was going to be Ballydoyle's

Derby horse that year. Ballydoyle and the Derby: it all seemed so impossibly glamorous. Maybe eight-year-olds, instead of pondering the inmates of a racing stable, should have been concentrating on more childish pursuits, but the memories remain as colourful as the Wibbly Wobbly Wonders we used to devour by the dozen.

I haven't spoken to Peter in thirty years but on this day, I think of him. Mind you, getting up at a quarter to five in the morning means it's an achievement in itself to numbly remember to put on pants before getting into the car for the long journey south to Tipperary. But any resentment at rising at such an ungodly hour is soon forgotten. After all, what would O'Shea give for the chance to plod around the world's most famous racing stable – and be able to pass it off as work? That's the happy fate in store for the fifty or so media types who pull up at Ballydoyle at eight in the morning for the annual press day. No one is allowed in until the appointed time so lines of cars spill out from the huge gates along each side of the Clonmel road, like the tentacles of some bleary eyed, petrol-guzzling jellyfish.

Security personnel eye the lot of us with undisguised suspicion while handing out name tags. With 140 racehorses inside, each of them with a pedigree to make Europe's monarchies resemble an underclass, it's hardly surprising that they're careful. At this time of year, when potential hasn't been soured by disappointment, it's estimated that there might be a €100 million worth of horseflesh in there. But it's still hard to quell the suspicion that some of it is for show: part of a deliberate attempt to create even more of an aura about the place.

When Vincent O'Brien started training at Ballydoyle in the 1950s, he knew well the appeal that exclusivity might have for his clients. Of course, the fact that he is the nearest the horse game has come to a genius helped too. At a time when the rest of Ireland was staring inwards, and not finding the view much to boast about, O'Brien was looking at the world and fancying his chances. And the little man from County Cork knew that no fishmonger ever made a penny by shouting stale fish.

The vision thing extended to his physical surroundings as much as himself. Today, the vision is provided by O'Brien's son-in-law, John Magnier. It was his original idea in the 1970s that the best way to make money from horses was to buy them as yearlings before their racing careers began, rely on O'Brien's talent to turn them into champions on the racecourse and then stand them at stud in Ireland where stallion income just happened to be tax free. From that germ, a colossal industry has sprouted, making Magnier extremely wealthy and also more than a little mysterious.

As usual, the man everybody in Coolmore calls Boss, and most everyone else in the horse business treats as God, is not here. Magnier reacts to media interest in him personally the way a hedgehog reacts to a large dog. It's not that he is averse to publicity, more that he is wary of bad publicity. Much of the Magnier enigma is that a considerable part of Coolmore's business is based on newspaper advertising and yet any personal contact with the press results in a display of porcupines that would have even the most ferocious media mutt howling for his mummy.

Instead, it is Aidan O'Brien who takes centre stage on

these annual press mornings. He is standing outside a massive barn inside which the first lot of fifty-two horses are already trotting, getting those expensive limbs warmed up in preparation for their morning workout. He has a handshake for everyone and makes a point of saying each name. These helpful tags don't seem to be necessary. The racing hack pack is a pretty homogenous group anyway, with the same faces showing up most years, but it's still pretty impressive that O'Brien can reel off all our names without missing a beat.

He is wired for sound, holding a large microphone with a pack tucked into his trouser belt. Even with that, everybody leans closer to him when he starts speaking. The only volume competition for the softly spoken trainer is the clicking of the horses' heels or an occasional rasp of teeth on a steel bit, and yet we circle around him as if he is about to unveil another secret from Fatima. No one wants to miss a little gem of information, so if O'Brien takes a few steps to inform one of the riders to pull a rug further up a horse's back or to do only one spin up the gallop instead of two, it looks like a slight, bespectacled whale is being tracked by a large shoal of some considerably over-nourished pilot fish.

Out on the gallop it is developing into one of those cold, sunlit spring mornings that can make this place look astonishingly lovely. In the distance, the rugged beauty of Slievenamon peeps through a slowly dissolving mist which lingers over the horses as they gallop towards us. It's as if all that muscular fluidity is on mute, because there is barely a sound from their hooves on the luxurious wood-shaving surface until they are almost past us. It could be an under-stated soundtrack for a sporting nursery sculpted by man out of a rural panorama that would still be recognisable to genera-tions before us. A lot of money is needed to maintain a place like this, but a lot of money never guarantees taste. John Magnier invests in art but the vision he probably really values is just a short car journey away from his Coolmore base. He's right too.

It's a Yeats that breaks the spell. There is a history of horses carrying that name in Ballydoyle and the latest, the five-year-old horse who won last year's Ascot Gold Cup, comes snorting towards us, making the sort of bellows-like racket you might expect if you of the visitors was asked to tackle the long, steep gradient.

'That's called flapping,' explains O'Brien. 'It's just his nostrils. You love to hear it because it means he's relaxed.'

There are nods from some of us, presumably in an attempt to give the impression that we knew that anyway. It's a dangerous tactic. There have been occasions here in the past when the name of a high-profile horse has been casually dropped and without a helpful steer from our host, lots of eyes have looked at lots of different animals. It's a fact some racing professionals have a problem coming to terms with – that scribbling for a paper does not mean the scribbler has to have an in-depth knowledge of the horse as a living-breathing creature in a stable. For most of us, the beast is simply a set of form figures and a handicap rating. Purists might be horrified but from the punting point of view, a field of bullocks could sweep around Tattenham Corner and it wouldn't matter just so long as it was possible to get a bet on.

The horses this morning are anything but bovine, however. Each of them is bred to win a Derby or a Guineas.

If one of them does, it constitutes a good year for their trainer: one more addition to the annual multimillion-dollar industry of Coolmore Stud. If none of them comes up to the mark, then being on the receiving end of God's baleful stare must feel like having been on the *Hood* when the *Bismarck*'s guns whirred into range. Considering the financial imperatives of getting it right, O'Brien seems to be remarkably relaxed.

Mind you, when he first came here in 1996, there weren't too many signs of him being on the verge of playing apples and oranges in the local health centre either. Being plunged into such a privileged and yet pressurised position means a natural inclination to keep his own counsel has been magnified, at least around those with biros ready to pounce. But there remains a natural civility to Aidan O'Brien that even colossal worldwide success hasn't altered. There is also, though, an almost oriental inscrutability. In public, at least, the mask never slips: enthusiasms are always kept in check. If O'Brien ever comes out with a statement along the lines of what the American trainer, Bud Delp, said about his 1979 Kentucky Derby winner, Spectacular Bid – 'the greatest horse ever to look through a bridle' – then it's safe to say the stewards will be ordering a dope test.

Disappointments are also dealt with behind this determined neutrality. Stories of an underlying temper do circulate but, by now, they have been mythologised to such an extent that your average Italian football manager resembles a hungover Bob Mitchum compared to when O'Brien apparently gets even slightly miffed.

In the absence of any independent confirmation of such wobbler tendencies, there is less sustaining fare for quote-hungry hacks to play with, something that, no doubt, places the trainer even closer to his master's bosom. But if there is one thing that can float O'Brien's boat out of neutral waters, it is a good horse. Over the past decade there have been plenty of those, and even though he has a commercial obligation to talk up his horses, even those that quite clearly can't move fast enough to get out of their own way, O'Brien's determinedly bland exterior still can't fully disguise genuine excitement at the idea of what the real top-notchers might do. He can't help it. All you have to do is recognise the signals and it can pay off spectacularly.

In the spring of 2002, for instance, the top-rated juvenile from the previous year was Johannesburg, a Breeders' Cup winner and the ante-post favourite for the Guineas, the Kentucky Derby and any other world classic you cared to mention. On the day we arrived, he was the horse that attracted most questions. But, significantly, it was another pair of colts, High Chaparral and Hawk Wing, who got their trainer all excited. High Chaparral, in particular, didn't have anything like Johannesburg's profile and yet, at the end, it was he and Hawk Wing that O'Brien picked for a now famous formal press-day photograph. Between them, the horses won seven Group 1 races. Johannesburg ran three times and never won again. Since then, O'Brien's photo picks deserve to be watched. Maybe it's a shrewd eye for future stallion brochures which motivates these snap sessions but it's preferable to think it's more a simple case of the man himself following his instincts.

It doesn't always work. In 2004, he talked about One Cool Cat in a way that quite frankly bordered on the erotic and that horse ended up beating only one horse home in the

2,000 Guineas. Last year, though, we were back to form with George Washington who earned a Coolmore career on the back of some mercurial brilliance that may at least be partly responsible for why he is now pooping from a great height on this year's party.

Nature's reminder that certitude and horses don't mate well means the classic ground has been swept from under O'Brien's feet. Halfway through the stud season, it has been discovered that behind all his swagger, George Washington happens to be just slightly more fertile than a sand trap. He has covered almost fifty mares and only a handful are in foal so the decision has been taken to take him out of Coolmore. But with breeders screaming for their mares to be impregnated, Magnier decides to take Holy Roman Emperor, his best racing prospect for 2007, out of Ballydoyle and press him into immediate stallion service. Apparently, the horse left Ballydoyle at eleven thirty in the morning and was on a mare by three that afternoon.

So, today, a couple of weeks later, O'Brien is without his best three-year-old and on top of that has to try and persuade the four-year-old George Washington to withdraw his fifth leg in return for getting his backside tanned in some more races.

'We have to teach him that he can't jump everything anymore,' the master trainer says balefully, sounding like Errol Flynn's agent might have if his man had been locked into a girls' convent school. 'Hopefully, we can get him back, please God.'

When O'Brien first came to prominence, his propensity for calling on the deity was such that he could hardly utter a sentence without throwing in a couple of 'please Gods'. He has cut down substantially but there is a definite murmur in the ranks when it emerges again, especially – it has to be said – among the cross-channel hacks. The cartoon representation of every Irish trainer as some twinkle-eyed trickster with a charming brogue and a love of sticking one on the poor, upstanding English across the water on the 'mainland' is always an easy option for some of the British guys. Right now, it's almost possible to hear some minds slipping into lazy gear, always a dangerous move around someone of substance.

O'Brien may come across as a shy country curate some-times, and he might often mangle some of the more grandiose names his horses are saddled with, but this is a man running a multimillion-euro operation whose success depends on his judgement being right more often than wrong. Every day brings decisions that can impact on a whole industry, whereas most of our big calls revolve around fiddling mileage expense claims.

There's no getting away from the impression, however, that with Holy Roman Emperor gone, O'Brien appears less than confident about the upcoming season. He reads through the list of horses and divides them into the usual 'possibles' for the Guineas and the Derby. Each ends up having about eight names. Even for Ballydoyle, it's impossible that they will all measure up. But the one word that sums up this operation is commercial. Everything has its price. Mentioning a horse in connection with a classic gives it currency, even if it ultimately never comes within a donkey's screech of Epsom or Newmarket. Potential buyers read papers too, after all.

What O'Brien and Magnier are banking on is one of them

turning into the real deal. One will do. He will pay for the others with more than a little to spare.

Of the horses with form, Mount Nelson and Duke Of Marmalade get favourable mention. Others, like Soldier Of Fortune and Macarthur, get put into the Derby class. But despite himself, O'Brien cannot help talking about how good Holy Roman Emperor might have been. The little colt spent his two-year-old career beating everything bar Teofilo, who is the red-hot ante-post favourite for this season's classics. They met twice and Teofilo won both times. O'Brien, however, sounds as if he was fancying his chances of third time lucky, and there's enough in his voice to suggest he isn't just plugging a stallion fee.

It's certainly enough to have us writing off any chance of a fifth O'Brien Guineas this year. He's just too downbeat. The usual script is being followed in terms of talking up the horses but, whatever about the words, the tone is all wrong. O'Brien almost admits as much, saying these horses need to find a lot of improvement to catch up. But most of us end up reckoning he doesn't think it's in them. Why else are there so many of last year's classic crop still around the place, including the Irish Derby winner, Dylan Thomas, and the top filly, Alexandrova? But if there aren't any classic goodies about the place, it still leaves a lot of creatures around here that will win a lot of races. Backing a 5–1 winner of the Derby might result in a warm glow of satisfaction at having your judgement backed on the biggest stage of all, but it pays off just the same as a 5–1 at a Wednesday evening gaff.

So, the usual habit of switching off while O'Brien talks about some of the lesser lights is reversed. Instead, he has to cope with an ear cocked so close to him he can count the number of hairs in it without even wanting to. Second lot pass by on their way back to the yard after exercise and the camera crews attempt to get a panoramic shot of the great trainer against the skyline while at the same time gesturing furiously for a large and apparently deaf reporter to get out of the way. Some chance: the only way O'Brien's getting some space is when the security guys are called.

Already, this heavy handed stalking has paid off. Apparently, a tall, grey filly called Diamond Necklace will leave her juvenile form well behind and the unnamed two-year-old son of High Chaparral and Mountain Holly has lots of pace.

It's good to hear, but hardly surprising. The one thing you will never hear from O'Brien is that something stays well. Stamina in a Coolmore stallion prospect is as popular as crabs on a troopship and so, for public consumption at least, every-thing that moves in Ballydoyle is fast. Even the trees grow quicker here. The crucial difference is in the inflection of O'Brien's words. When he's serious about a sure-fire future maiden winner, his tone tends to drop slightly, and he delivers a rather meaningful look to whomever's nearest to him. By practically sitting in his lap, the name of a promising filly called Peeping Fawn and another unnamed two-year-old by Kingmambo have been secured.

It's then that a large bay colt steps past, ears pricked with interest at the mob around him, but totally calm. His attitude is inquisitive rather than panicky, which is hardly surprising. After all, we're on his patch. Even to a non-expert, he looks magnificent. There's an undeniable presence to him.

'What's that horse, Aidan?'

'He's a Galileo, out of Rainbow Goddess. A three-year-old: hasn't raced yet. A fine-looking horse, isn't he?'

As the last of the string walk past, O'Brien's register drops. 'He could be anything.'

My 'informant' walks off after his horses, followed by the pack, which is down one member. A frantic scan of the list finds the mare's name, Rainbow Goddess. Her son is called Mahler. As Trish says in *Educating Rita*, 'Wouldn't you just die without Mahler?' Right now, I just might.

Running total: - €100

Will Perv For Money

7 April

The success of the internet betting company Betfair is at least partly due to how easy it is to join it. After just ten minutes online, and in spite of a tortuously slow broadband system, I've become a new member of the world's most revolutionary betting community. Five minutes later, only some frantic pawing of the keyboard prevents Essendon getting laid for €500 against another Australian Rules football team called the Kangaroos.

It's not an encouraging start but there is nothing for it but to persevere. There are still plenty of punters who distrust internet betting as a bewildering, unpoliced badland and who don't go near the exchanges on principle. But that attitude is quickly becoming akin to those who resolutely rode to work while munching on the muck thrown up by Henry Ford's Model-Ts. There's no going back. Last year, a Japanese company purchased 23 per cent of Betfair at a price that valued the company at £1.5 billion. That sort of figure doesn't allow for nostalgia.

The central theory of the betting exchanges is so blindingly obvious it makes you want to gnaw the table with frustration that you didn't think of it first. Basically, the idea is that there is no real need for a bookmaker, like Paddy Power or Ladbrokes. Instead, the customer can be a bookmaker as well as a punter. All that matters is getting someone that fancies a horse to win to make contact with someone who believes that the beast will lose. Then, let them trade and haggle and negotiate on their own. Do that and there's no need for hiking to a betting shop and scrawling out a betting docket. All anyone needs is a computer and a credit card and it is Caesar's Palace in the comfort of your own home – except without the free drinks.

But, although the exchanges pride themselves on being customer-friendly, there is no point in believing that everyone is going to play the system like a virtuoso from the off. At first, it can be quite intimidating. When called up, each race, or match or event, pretty much fills the screen with a massive selection of figures that resembles a stock exchange. Apparently, that is deliberate because whether it is betting on football, racing, the Eurovision Song Contest or the width of Posh Spice's waist, the idea is to treat the business very much in the same manner as you would if you were trading in stocks and shares. There is also the fact that making it seem businesslike enables customers feel less guilty about deliberating for hours on end about the possible outcome of a football match.

It isn't long, though, before a rather less-grandiose way of explaining how the system works comes to mind. At either end of the screen, and running inwards are the prices at which both the better and the layer are willing to do business. In the middle are the best prices available to bet or lay. Anyone who has ever gone through the tortuous waltz of bid and counterbid when buying or selling a house will recognise it straight away – except that here finding a figure that suits both sides can take just seconds. Practise, however, is important. To prevent Essendon being doubled with the Wagga Wagga ladies' bowls team, some midnight fumbling is called for.

At first, it takes an effort not to draw the curtains. There's nothing wrong with something so natural, of course – but still. With the wife and kids tucked up in bed asleep, there is something undeniably illicit – maybe even a little grubby – about sitting in the dark with only the laptop's glow and a barely audible television for company. After all, it's not like watching the rampant, free-to-view soft porn that seems to be on every other channel after ten o'clock. Instead, while the rest of honest-to-God mankind is perving out to the plastic-boobed grind of the barely knickered, yours truly is glued to the attheraces channel.

Even a decade ago, it was unthinkable that racing of any kind might be available at home through the night like this. Satellite technology, however, has smashed the boundaries. Today, after the horses have stopped running in Ireland and Britain, they kick into gear in the US, and when that's finished, the world spins us into the delights of Australia. With the exchanges open twenty-four hours a day, it's now possible to bet around the clock and around the globe.

So, rather like a middle-aged Holden Caulfield and his fateful hotel date, this is an opportunity to use American and Australian racing to practise. Improve technique, if you like: just a tenner in each race in order to feel comfortable with the technology. The horses and jockeys and their form are a total mystery but playing hunches for small money can be fun. And there is also the not-inconsiderable bonus of not having to slap the kids and/or wife away from the television when they demand to watch something else. Pretty soon, those first tentative stabs at the keyboard, usually accompanied by anxious glances at the screen to see if a bailiff has seen his cue, disappear in a blur of digital speed. After all, there's a mud-loving filly with a bellyful of lasix who's on top of the rail bias at Forrest Gump Falls and just has to be bet.

The American stuff really is a different world from racing here. Even language gets cut up in the cultural mangle. In the US, a speed horse is one that leads: here, it is the one coming from the back. 'Off' refers to a track that's wet whereas it has rather more colourful connotations on this side of the puddle.

But the unfamiliarity is good. This isn't what the season is going to be about at all. It's just play. It is three nights of play that results in being down €200, but the consolation is in knowing this is only a phoney war. There will be time enough to drive a punting Panzer through those massed ranks of bookmakers nearer to home. Form at this time of year has to settle down. As wet going turns faster with the better weather, form lines can switch around spectacularly. Some horses can rattle off quick ground with aplomb. Others can hardly walk on it without flinching, like Ian Paisley padding through a friary. What's important, right now, is to formulate a strategy.

I lodge a grand with Betfair. The rest is kept for more traditional warfare with the bookmakers. And even though it might not have been obvious to anyone peeping through the curtain, there is one vital codeword that will underpin the whole enterprise. Read any betting book, or listen to the experts, and the one mantra they repeat over and over again is that 'discipline' is everything. Playing hunches is what mugs do – to make it pay, you have to be disciplined.

Metaphorically, there is already a coat of arms above the desk, a Rubenesque nymph clutching a stubby bookie-shop pencil in one hand and a cat-o'-nine-tails in the other. Sometimes, as another tenner goes down the pan at Redneck Downs, she appears to pull those black thigh boots up even higher towards that studded corset with its spiked pelt of dead dockets…

The indulgence of Day One at the Curragh and of three nights messing on the sofa means there is €4,700 left in the pot. This is faithfully recorded. If that seems the action of a man with an excessively puckered rectum, then it's only fair to inform you of my underlying impulsive nature which is more than capable of finding a 10–1 shot and chancing its arm on an all-or-nothing gamble. Reining in such recklessness is vital.

A hundred will be the minimum stake. That allows for a maximum of forty-seven bets, or forty-seven points. The scale of confidence will rise from there. A 'mortal lock', as the yee-haw merchants in the States describe a racing certainty, might mean a five-point bet. Any more than that will be proof that the plot is being well and truly lost. Talking about points rather than money is also likely to prevent a leap from altitude when things go wrong. But such fears are fleeting. Instead, there is enough of that start-of-term optimism still around to arouse nothing but impatience for the real green light to shine. And, today, it finally does. Mahler has his first race at Leopardstown.

If you read enough of the overseas racing press, it can sometimes seem that being Irish earns everyone a free pass into the horsey-club. That usually manifests itself in lines about 'the whole of Ireland' being on some favourite at the Cheltenham festival. The truth is that the whole of Ireland mostly couldn't give a good goddam for any favourite at Cheltenham or anywhere else. In fact, the vast majority of the country has never been at a race meeting at all. A perfect example arrives in the form of a cousin, Karen, her husband, Rory, and their three kids, who are visiting for Easter.

'You know what? I've never been racing in my life,' Karen announces at breakfast.

'Same here,' Rory adds.

Taking them is perfect cover for being at the races and not working. Other options for explaining a rare Saturday at the track include telling the truth, but marines jumped ashore at Okinawa with lighter hearts than I have at the idea of informing some of my colleagues about what's going on. If you believe that to be a little insecure, then you're right. We are talking some good friends here, top people, whose ability to take the piss should have had them signed as consultants by the colostomy bag industry years ago. We are also talking a level of cynicism that really does mean they would look around for the coffin if they smelled some flowers. For morale's sake alone, avoiding telling the truth on this matter for a little while is important. The problem now, however, is that this convenient cover is causing a delay.

By the time nappies are changed, puke wiped away and kids organised, we've only twenty-five minutes to make the first race where Diamond Necklace, the big grey filly that Aidan predicted would do much better this year, is due to run. She's a 7–1 shot for a maiden. That's the sort of price to burn some rubber for. But burning rubber presumes a certain velocity and the M50 is not playing ball. Karen & Co. are treated to the sight of 'Uncle Brian' doing a turkey cock of splenetic fury as the traffic slowly spews its way around the city. An eyes-down, buttock-clenched charge up the emergency lane eventually gets us off the four-lane car park and brings us speeding to the back of the queue snaking its way towards Leopardstown's front gates.

This is maddening, and there's no room to try and pull a dodge. A T-34 couldn't carve its way out of this jam. There's nothing for it but to sit. Just as we eventually manage to turn right into the course, the race is off.

Listening to the RTÉ radio commentary, while trying not to think of one point at 7–1, and ignoring the whispers in the back pointing out the rather large pulsing vein that apparently has decided to visit the back of my skull, it takes an effort not to wish Diamond Necklace some serious ill will. It would be just typical if she wins. Just the sort of start that's required. As we snake up the long avenue, alongside the finishing straight, the runners suddenly and dramatically are no more than a couple of hundred of yards away. Diamond Necklace is unmistakable, that grey frame angling for a run towards the lead. The faint thud of the whips starting to strike reach over the engines and the course commentary: it's inevitable that she is going to win.

But she doesn't: she doesn't even make the first three. Instead, the other O'Brien runner, All My Loving, comes out on top at a longer price than her stable companion and I feel enough relief to make it feel like I backed a winner. This is a good sign, like something is meant to be. If Diamond Necklace had won, it would cast a pall. Like some higher power saying, 'Not today, pal.' That's completely illogical, of course, but whoever came to a racetrack for logic? So, instead of being escorted around by a mad, mystic mullah of doom, the racing virgins are being steered by a comparatively light-hearted guide.

It's an interesting experience looking at a race meeting through the eyes of newcomers. When you're not working, the time between races really starts to lag, especially when you're trying to stop the kids from complaining about being bored. Introducing both Ben and Eve to the delights of the Tote and the burger van keeps them occupied for the first two races, but hanging around in front of the stands watching the world go by eventually starts to lose its appeal for them. And this is on a wonderfully sunny afternoon: trying to keep the whine levels to an acceptable level in the rain would not be fun.

'I can see how it could be a good day out,' Karen concludes. 'But you'd need to leave the kids at home – and be able to drink. There's nothing else to do, really, is there?'

It's time to park this social experiment for a while, though. The third race is a seven-furlong handicap that features two horses that ran on Day One at the Curragh. Out Of The Red had Warriors Key a length behind him when he was runner-up to his stable companion, Little White Lie. Afterwards, the winning trainer said the second would be better on faster ground. Out Of The Red has got that now, and his jockey should be capable of a better ride this time. At 4–1, he looks a reasonable bet. He is too – a perfectly reasonable each way bet. Out Of The Red travels like a winner for most of the race and fifty yards from the line, it looks over. But then, Warriors Key suddenly finds another burst and nails his rival on the line by a short head.

Each way betting has never floated my boat. Paying the win and then the place just seems like doubling the bet. The sober argument is that it provides a dig out if things don't turn out ideally but that probably comes down to a temperament thing – and this temper believes that if you fancy the horse, you just put your head down and go for it. Each way is the bet your accountant would advise, and who ever depended on an accountant for thrills?

There's certainly no each way option for Mahler. The Drumderrry Maiden, run over a mile-and-a-quarter, might be worth just €11,747 to the winner but that's only a fraction of what some of these three-year-olds could be worth. Early-season maidens at the big tracks are always competitive but, from the gossip in the ring and around the weigh room, at least four horses are expected to win. Mahler will start as favourite. Another unraced O'Brien colt by Galileo called Acapulco made his debut at Navan a weekend ago and skated up by nine lengths. Normally, these newcomers need their first run. But Acapulco didn't, and Mahler is reputed to be at least as good. The good news is that with Mores Wells, Mourilyan and a raw gangling beast called Vincenzio Galilei also supposed to be the nearest thing to Pegasus incarnate, there's no danger of Mahler being a ridiculously short favourite.

It's always a good idea to examine the saddling box area. Considering the parade ring is only yards away, and people are spilling back from the front of the stands, it's remarkably peaceful. Not too many come here to lean on the rail and watch this behind-the-scenes tranquillity. They're missing out. The sun is warm enough to be pleasant and a breeze rustles through the oak trees overlooking the line of magnolia-painted stables. It looks like a pretty miniature terrace of suburban orderliness, until a scrape of a hoof or a moving shadow in the gloom betrays an occupant. There is very little said as the runners are led around in front of the boxes. Some are saddled up already. But the three Ballydoyle runners are bare-backed and waiting.

Mahler looks the pick of them by some way. That lordly attitude from a few weeks ago isn't quite as pronounced but the idea that a new experience like this might cause him to get on edge is not a concern. Instead, he saunters around, head low, appreciating the sun on his back, and appearing not to have a care in the world. It's a great sign. To his left, Red Kingdom, a 100–1 outsider, is on his toes and spookily pointing his head towards the sky as a possible escape route.

O'Brien arrives and begins his pre-race ritual. It's the same at Epsom for the Derby or Tipperary for a maiden. The horse is held by one of the lads and the master horseman puts a reassuring hand along its withers and back. The rubber pad on which the saddle will sit goes on first, followed by the number-cloth, and then the postage stamp of a saddle. The girths are swung underneath the horse's belly and handed to a crouching O'Brien who pulls hard to tighten them before one final check to see that the saddle is sitting right. Then he gives the mane and tail a final brush out and sponges the horse's mouth with water. Sometimes, one of them will require a leg-stretch, where both front limbs are stretched out in front, rather like a footballer warming up. It's a strange thing to see at first. You would think the animal's first reaction to such an unnatural position would be to lash out, but O'Brien can make it look no more unusual than a father ruffling a child's hair.

Mahler's mood doesn't change and he plods around the parade ring like an old steeplechaser rather than a three-year-old colt. Along with the rest of the field, he emerges from the chute out to the track and canters to the start just as I get 5–2 from a bookmaker. At this moment, for a horse that 'could be anything', the price looks like a gift from the gods. The original plan to ease into things with a one-point bet has disappeared. Out Of The Red had been a one pointer. It's time to bet properly. Four points will get a grand. It sounds good.

At the start, Mahler walks into his stall as if he's been doing it all his life. He's 9–4 now with the bookies, which means I've got a small edge already. As the last of them load up, my heart feels like it is plugged into a jack-hammer. For once, there is no large screen in front of the stands, so a TV in the bookies' ring is the best option and a group of us pack around.

My horse – and by now it feels like I have at least an equal share with John Magnier – breaks perfectly well and sits in third or fourth for the first furlong. His jockey, Seamus Heffernan, doesn't look anxious as Mourilyan makes ground to take the lead. Mahler loses a position on the outside but, again, Heffernan appears unconcerned. There's a mile to go: plenty of time left. Mahler isn't exhibiting the usual keenness to get on with things that often blights a horse's first race. The sickening realisation that he doesn't appear keen to do any-thing much at all doesn't come until another couple of furlongs. He slips back to second last and Heffernan starts tapping him down the shoulder with his whip. He may as well be tapping the *Ark Royal* for all the response it generates. Mahler is clearly as green as grass. He looks like he barely knows how to gallop forward. They haven't even made the straight and it's obvious there's no chance. Nothing can win from there.

Karen, Rory and the kids charge the gates on the way out. We leave before the last to beat the traffic. The small ones have the exultantly relieved faces one imagines the Mafeking lookouts had when Mahon marched over the horizon. Their driver no doubt resembles Cronje after looking behind him. Nothing much is said until we hit the M50 again. Then Karen pipes up.

'It isn't my cup of tea, I have to say. But it really is a relax-ing way to spend an afternoon.'

Running total: - €800

Me and Warren Beatty

6 May

The scientific term is 'spooked'. Call it naïvety or simplicity or even raving arrogance, but the idea of reaching into minus figures hadn't occured to me. There would be stretches when things wouldn't go right, that much was obvious. Even Warren Beatty has had dry periods, apparently. Yet he will always and forever be the man who rolled off Natalie Wood and on to Julie Christie. His reputation is cast-iron. Some of us don't have that kind of safety net.

Almost a fifth of the pot is already gone and the nearest thing to a winner has been Out Of The Red whose name increasingly feels like an ironic kick in the privates. Suddenly, the end of the season in November seems an awfully long way away. Will there even be a pot a month from now? Will the experiment die without leaving the Petri dish?

This you will recognise as the bracing gust of reality whistling around an exposed arse, which, right now, seems to be hanging out farther than a whaler's harpoon. What was curiosity is starting to turn into a very public display of inadequacy. A substantial consolation for getting it wrong for a newspaper is that it will be mostly forgotten by the next day. But this doozy of an idea will be in cold, unforgiving print for a lot longer than that – a bald, black-and-white monument to bad judgement.

These are the thoughts that tag along through the weeks when the jump game takes over again. First, the three days of the Easter Festival at Fairyhouse, followed in the same week by three days in Liverpool for the Grand National. That's just perfect: nothing a person with the willies needs more than a stay in Scouseville. If you ever want to know why The Beatles took so enthusiastically to mind-altering substances, then simply stare through the drizzle across the 'Merrrr-sey' to 'Biirrkkhhenn-ead' or the 'Wiiiiiirrrallllll' and ponder the advantages of getting the hell out.

Maybe that's harsh, but now doesn't feel like a time for qualifications. Anyway, the vast majority of the British hacks anticipate this week with all the relish Paul reserves for John's missus, and they know a lot more about what the rest of this country is like. There are areas near the docks that look like the Luftwaffe is still coming over at night. Those of us who remember Dublin before the Celtic Tiger immediately recognise the neglect and decay of areas that could be rolled up and sold to Angola without anyone missing them for days.

And, of course, there's the 'akkkhhh-sunt' which stubbornly refuses to loosen its grip even weeks after getting home, and can make ordering a cup of coffee sound like the final gasps of a hundred-a-day consumptive.

For the record, it must be pointed out that thousands of Irish racegoers plan their year around the Grand National and think Liverpool is the home of all things bright and beautiful. And there's no denying that it does have its moments – many of them, as it happens, on the train from Aintree back to the city after the racing is over. Piled in tighter than a backpacker's underwear, the overwhelming smell of drink is always a good indication of the levels of raucous enjoyment, particularly from the women. Kitted out in their best dental floss, regardless of weather, they bring a direct charm to the subject of all matters sexual, usually at ear-splitting volume. This year, the highlight is supplied by a young woman leafing through the racecard until arriving at a page advertising the forthcoming appearance of the smouldering soul singer, Lemar. 'Jeeee-ssuus,' she announces to the carriage, while suggestively trailing a finger down the page. 'I'd give him such a fuccckkhhin!'

OK, O'Brien had said Mahler was a 'could be anything' but that didn't rule out the possibility of the horse being a lazy tramp. So, where is the glory in blindly following a throw-away remark and having almost a maximum bet on with not one iota of form to go on? Everyone knows the benefit every horse gets from having a run. Only the rare ones go in first time. Expecting Mahler to not fluff his lines was like sending a child to his first morning in school and expecting him to recite the *Iliad* in the afternoon.

It's time to get real. Mahler was little more than another

hunch bet. From now on, reason has to apply. By definition, logic can't be applied to something so cerebral but if there has to be a guess, then it has to be an educated guess. At least if it loses there won't be the guilt of suspecting that all the bases hadn't been covered. It's time to be professional about it. So, armed with this resolution, I spend an hour before racing each day putting together some combination bets.

Aintree is a jumps meeting so the money isn't coming from the betting pool. That's the excuse anyway for a series of accumulators and yankees that invariably end up in the media-room bins. These are the kinds of bets that keep the bookmaking industry in cream. Every so often, one will come off and will be turned into the sort of free publicity that would otherwise cost a fortune. But the more names that appear on a slip, the more chances there are for the bet to fail. It's mug punting, only just short of filling out a lottery ticket.

It only emphasises the need to be serious about this. Just because something isn't life or death doesn't mean it's frivolous. Playing football is a ridiculous way for a grown man to make a living but nobody ever accused Roy Keane of being anything but serious.

Unfortunately, some of us seem incapable of following our own advice. After the leaving of Liverpool, and the resultant shedding of tears, a family expedition to Copenhagen takes four days. Five hours before we arrive back in Dublin airport, all refreshed and relaxed from travelling with two small kids on a small Ryanair plane from an even smaller dot of an airport in Sweden, Mahler leads all the way to win at Leopardstown. He's a 5–2 favourite. I didn't even know he was running. Denmark is hardly some technological backwater – it is even possible to get online there – but holiday mode took over. Off is off, after all. Except, in this lark, nobody can afford to switch off completely. Mahler would have been backed again – probably out of stubbornness, which is hardly the best reason to do anything, and certainly not for four points, but still. As omens go, it ain't great. And after this, things start to go even further downhill.

It's not as if there isn't any work going into this. My job entails looking at form anyway but hours of study are now going into it. Old and much beloved shortcuts are being ignored. There is always the temptation, especially in a rush, to have a quick look over the card and let first impressions pick out your seven horses, which is actually no barrier to getting it right.

That might offend the more puritanical but the one and only time I have picked every winner on a card came from just such a tactic. Soon after beginning work for the *Irish Press*, carelessness resulted in no tips for a nondescript meeting at Tralee and a summons back to the office. Grumbling at the disruption to a liver-pickling contest in Mulligan's pub, said Tralee card got the sort of attention it deserved – juggling the first and second-favourites in the probable starting price sections at the bottom of each race. It was only when I was watching the TV news the following evening that the names of that day's winners started to ring a bell. A quick glance at the paper confirmed the 1,432–1 fluke: seven out of seven. Sure enough, the next day's edition had a blurb, accompanied by a photo of a slightly shamefaced hack staring sphinx-like from the back page, proclaiming the *Irish Press* as the home of the winners. A year later, the place closed down.

But there's nothing like that going on now. Armed with a *Turform* annual, the anorak's must-have accessory, and access to the limitless form records of the *Racing Post* website, as well as irish-racing.com, every runner gets the sort of attention that my previous *Irish Press* incarnation would have ridiculed.

The next day's runners come out before eleven in the morning and it's head down straight away. Irish-racing.com has a nifty little feature that reveals each runner's previous two bits of form in a little box when you hold the cursor over its name. An hour gives a pretty accurate impression of the races and who the contenders are likely to be. Final jockeys are declared before one o'clock, revealing the full picture. Then the real study begins. Armed with a laptop, there is now no excuse for not knowing the form and pedigree of every nag that has ever set foot on a racecourse anywhere in the world. It's all there, but it also takes time and when you're not getting any results for all this work, it can be a bit of a drag. Clearly, we're not talking drudgery of the down-the-pit variety but, after weeks of earnest study, a certain conclusion has to be drawn.

John Merrick had a better strike rate with the ladies. That vital sense of judgement as to what constitutes a reasonable bet and what doesn't is fatally off-kilter. A horse like Flash McGahon runs in a Listed race at Cork after finishing second to Dandy Man, possibly the fastest horse in Europe right now, and manages to beat only one home. Another point disappears on Peeping Fawn at Gowran after getting over twice her 15–8 starting price on Betfair. Then, when it appears to be spot on, say with two fillies at Navan who sluice up, I back neither because the prices are too short.

The result is nostalgia for that happy week in Liverpool. By the time of the Guineas at Newmarket, the points theory is well and truly shot to smithereens. Losing €100 a bet is too much. My morale can't take it. So the basic is dropped to €70, then to €50. It isn't long before it feels better not to have a bet at all. Even approaching the *Racing Post* in the morning becomes a tentative exercise. Losing like this is just too depressing. It's a statistical fact that almost a third of all favourites win. But, even in the midst of this funk, it is obvious that lumping blindly on a series of odds-on shots is not the way to go, even though the physical act of backing a winner would be the sort of novelty that getting a banana in 1945 must have been.

What is genuinely unsettling, though, is that the dispiriting impact of all this is starting to accumulate. Apparently, for the last few weeks, an angry Alex Ferguson in full 'hairdryer' mode would have been a more agreeable husband than the morose, mumbling neurotic who has been prowling the house. The verdict is a little harsh, but only a little. Even minor hiccups are provoking operatic reactions: a fuse blowing in the pump-house provokes a face like a smacked arse. The baby puking on a suit just before going to the races results in notes that Maria Callas couldn't hit.

'Is this really worth it?' coos my gentler-half soothingly. 'You're really starting to get on my tits.'

The atmosphere isn't helped by the first classics of the season A speculative €50 on Dutch Art in the 2,000 Guineas comes agonisingly close to paying off but the field split into two groups and he is on the wrong side and gets done by a length. Finsceal Beo is a red-hot favourite for the 1,000 and, from what we hear about her homework, it is only a matter of going down and coming back. That's the sort of information to stiffen even the most flaccid loin and the morning is taken up by wondering whether or not to take the generally available 5–2 or wait to see what happens in the afternoon. There are twenty lining up against her. At least a couple of them will have improved spectacularly over the winter. It's always the way with fillies. It demands at least 3–1 to play. Instead the 5–2 is snapped up and Finsceal Beo ends up a 5–4 favourite which is way too short. Logic says she's not a bet at those odds, and logic farts loudly as she dots up by three lengths. It's obvious throughout that the vibes about Finsceal were, if anything, understating the case. Not for one moment does she look like losing, and, remarkably, it doesn't matter a damn.

The fourth and final leg of a €10 accumulator – the sort that only mugs do, and the result of a fatalistic few minutes spent in a bookie's office in the morning – is about to run. It's still an effort to even believe we've got to this stage. But if this one comes in, there's a €1,100 pay-off waiting. It will be enough to cover everything lost up to now, and even leave some spare change. The prospect is enough to provoke blubbering gratitude and more than a little shame. Accumulator's are pathetic, a one-way train to Bum Junction: and nobody will ever be more grateful for one coming up.

It's only a result of having gone into a shop to see their Finsceal Beo odds. Being armed with a short, stumpy biro in such a place can be dangerous and, without even realising it, the names of three horses were suddenly on a slip. There wasn't even a conscious decision to do it. They seemed to write themselves – Kyle in the first race at Salisbury, Lipocco in the second and Sixties Icon in the Jockey Club Stakes at Newmarket. Sixties Icon is a St Leger winner but the other two are shots in the dark, except that Kyle is trained by Richard Hannon who has a great record around Salisbury, and Lipocco has the best jockey at the meeting in Seb Sanders. Amazingly, the non-forensic approach is working.

Kyle has to get a few thumps to win but Lipocco wins almost as easily as Sixties Icon who has Frankie Dettori doing gymnastics in the saddle. He looks arthritic compared to at least one desperate hack a few hundred miles to the west.

Now it all comes down to the last leg, which, in a freaky-karma and too-weird-to-make-up way, fits perfectly. He's only on the docket because of the last day and through a desperate cosmic yearning to believe he owes, which only shows how low things have gone. It's a sure sign that doom is around the corner when bargains are being struck with a greater power than the formbook. But there it is – Mahler has it in him to break my heart twice in a month. Please, Jesus, let him win.

Mahler's running in a mile-and-a-half race at Gowran that is billed as a classic trial and which has also attracted his old friend, Vincenzio Galilei. He finished well ahead last month but it's very different now. The Mahler of last month has been transformed. Heffernan isn't going to allow any messing around and goes straight to the lead. It's too fanciful to say out loud but there's something so wonderfully fluid about the display that it feels like watching a great poem hit every beat on the button on the way to a perfect finale. Mahler has everything at it early in the straight and by the furlong pole, he is three lengths clear. At the line, he wins by five with his ears flicking around and looking like he could do it all again. Even the very idea would have me on a drip.

A quick tot of his 4–5 odds-on to the other three brings up €1,111. It just about brings things back to square one. Financial respectability has been restored – just. Even in the midst of this euphoria and relief, there is still no getting away from a little voice preaching that reliance on this sort of blatant jamminess is a one-way ticket to Palookaville. Judgement lost out to good fortune today but judgement will always back itself to win overall. But for the moment, God bless you Gustav, you big, beautiful bastard.

Running total: + €71.50

My Vibrating Virgil

9 May

Let's call him Virgil, as in Steve McQueen's character in *The Great Escape*. Like Steve, there's a barely contained restlessness to him. He practically dances with impatience, eyes darting every which way, phone switching from hand to hand, while I try to pump him for wisdom. As we stand in a racecourse hallway, the distinct impression emerges that, right now, this Virgil Hilts would clear any kind of wire to get away. Maybe it's because there is a raging-hot good-thing going in the next race – or maybe it's his normal demeanour. The overall impact though is kind of cool. It's clearly on the tip of his tongue to tell this unwanted ferret to get back in his hole but, like the Cooler King himself, he manfully manages to swallow his irritation – for a while, anyway.

He's Virg because he doesn't want his real name to be used. That's understandable. Making a living from betting the horses is hardly a spectator sport, and the less the Revenue Commissioners know, the better. A mutual friend has set up the meeting. It has quickly become apparent that trying to hatch this project in a private incubator is a sure-fire way to financial disaster, so a quiet shriek in the ear of a colleague has resulted in an audience with someone who actually knows what he's talking about. Virg shows up, looking around as if the searchlights are about to pick him out.

'Thanks a lot for doing this,' I say. 'Fancy a drink or a cup of coffee?'

'No. What do you want to know?'

Only the secret to betting nirvana – but maybe now isn't the time to try and lighten the mood. His foot starts tapping a skirting board like he's trying to get some dirt from the escape tunnel out of his trouser leg. Looking at this perpetual motion is enough to make you queasy, like staring out of a Tokyo skyscraper during an earthquake. There's also the fact that he isn't quite the figure I expected. He's young, and there are few things better for middle-aged morale than admitting to a pup that you need help. It could be worse though. Young he may be, but a sober suit and grey overcoat suggest the weighty bearing of a Turf Club steward. The overcoat looks reassuringly expensive too.

A brief explanation of my adding-a-zero ambition is enough to provoke a smile. That's enough to stop Tokyo shaking for a while. The smile isn't cruel or snide, it's more indulgent than that – the kind you give a toddler when they wet themselves during toilet training.

'You don't think it's a runner, then?' I simper.

'Oh, I don't know about that. How're you doing so far?'

The coat alone says Virg has been doing a hell of a lot better, and for a lot longer too. This is his living after all. He reckons there might be forty others like him, fifty max, making the betting game pay in this country. When you hear commentators on TV mentioning a horse being backed by the 'right faces', it is Virg & Co. they're talking about. Some trade as bookmakers too, but that's very much a sideline to some serious punting. They're following the method of J.P. McManus who years ago concluded that having to offer a price as a bookie on every horse in every race doesn't make financial sense when a punter only needs one horse at the right price. These are the guys at the coal face, where the stark bottom line of solvency decides if they are any good or not. It makes sense, then, to try and tease out some wisdom from one of this rare breed.

'What do you go on most?' I ask. 'Form or information?'

Virg looks pityingly, it doesn't matter. Being on a drier streak than a Bedouin naturist has banished all thoughts of ego.

'Anyone relying on form can't do this,' he declares simply.

'But I've been busting my hump for hours every day looking up formbooks and computers.'

'So?'

So, indeed. Knowing the form backwards is basic enough to dismiss even being mentioned. It's like the interview board for a solicitor's job presuming everyone coming in has a law degree – or, possibly more apt, it's like an actor researching a part, spending months swotting up on every little stitch of a life, and then throwing it all out in order to let the relevant stuff emerge through the character. Except such cerebral comparisons are not really Virg's thing.

'Maybe you can get away with just knowing the form in somewhere like America where all the tracks are the same shape and times mean something. But what does Ballinrobe have in common with Downpatrick? Fuck all – except bad horses. They might all have their day, one day, but trying to figure out when it'll be is impossible, unless you're getting good information.'

It quickly becomes apparent there's enough information coming Virg's way to make him the Bletchley Park of the betting ring. Having worked with horses in the past, he has the considerable advantage of being 'in' with a seemingly huge number of people. There's more flesh being pressed than during a general election – and Virg is no politician desperately looking for hands to shake. Instead, a series of jockeys, trainers, owners, punters and priests almost line up to confess their sins to him. It is little wonder the guy was so edgy earlier. He's like a squirrel collecting info for the winter: there's only so much time that can be wasted.

No doubt there are conspiracy theorists who will view such encounters with a bleary eye and mutter about corruption and sharp practice. In racing's complex vernacular, there is no more loaded word than 'information'. Its meaning can run from casual chat to a sinister set-up. Only the hopelessly naïve can believe that there isn't a whole lot of money changing hands between punters, bookies and racing professionals in order to get an edge. It has always been so and, barring a mass turning to organised religion, it always will be.

But tarring everyone with that brush is misleading. Sometimes 'information' really does consist of pals jawing and nothing else. In fact, for most punters, 'information' consists of minor bits of rumour and gossip that add up to a big picture – such as, who has improved a lot for their last run, who hasn't come on at all, which stable has a touch of the virus, or the horse in the last who's handicapped at shorter distances and is really a stayer. There's certainly no quick exchange of cash right now between Virgil and anyone else. And even if it isn't all above board, how can anyone prove it? Maybe there is some furtive envelope swapping away from the racecourse, or an extravagant Christmas present at the end of the year, but is anyone really surprised by that? Does anyone believe the same doesn't happen between GPs and consultants? Or that a hell of a lot more iffy stuff goes on between government and big business? Virg is careful, though, to keep his bullshit detector on at full-blast the whole time.

'I'm here only an hour and already I've had fellas coming up to me and telling me such and such is fancied, blah, blah. But you learn to weed out the bullshitters,' he says. 'It's like jockeys. A jockey will tell you anything. Most of them are desperate at tipping a winner. You name a horse they're riding and they'll say, "Yeah, yeah, I've a chance." And you know they haven't a snowball's.'

Even a brief tag-along around the racecourse is enough to know it will do no harm to listen to what Virg has to say. There's a resolute purpose to the way he strides to the betting ring, phone clamped to an ear, pausing to talk to yet another 'informant'. The man looks as completely at home in this environment as Mick Kinane does a hundred yards away out on the track. Plus, it doesn't take long to warm to the guy. Clearly, he's no soft touch but he has also, so far, resisted the urge to tell the large shadow beside him to 'fuck off', and there's a sardonic sense of humour there that's easy to like.

'I love money. We all do. But I love quick money. And backing horses is a way to make dough quick. It's actually not very hard to get a few quid out of it. There are a lot harder ways to make a living!'

This is what it's supposed to be like. Playing the game the way it's supposed to be played.

'What's your system?' I ask.

'My what?'

'Your system: you know, do you do the points thing? Like so much equals one point and you don't bet more than so many points.'

'No, I don't,' he snorts. 'I just do whatever comes along.'

'But what about everyone going on about betting with discipline?'

'Fair enough, you can't go mad all the time,' he grins. 'But everyone gets carried away sometimes. You have to have a bit of fun.'

Virg's one constant is that he goes to every race meeting – every flat meeting that is. The jumps are too unreliable – mug punting. At the races you hear stuff, and you get to see the horses in the parade ring. Combine what you hear and see with what you believe, and you have all the ingredients for a bet.

'I bet between €50 and €500. It's very rare I go beyond that. I wouldn't bet every race but it wouldn't bother me to bet a couple of times a day.'

'Can I take notes?'

'I don't know,' he grins. 'Can you?'

Virg is starting to loosen up. Partly, no doubt, out of pity for the harmless hanger-on who's so obviously out of his depth, but also, probably, because this only reinforces his belief that he's got things pretty sorted – 'Tell me any nine-to-five job that's this good!'

Systems are not Virg's thing. They're too much like work. It's why he only opens a Betfair account for the Cheltenham festival in March and immediately closes it when the four days are up.

'I've no interest in laying horses anyway, but it's the most tedious way to spend a day, sitting in front of a computer like that. You'll make money all right, betting the figures and the margins like you're playing the markets. But I make money my way too, and I'll bet I have more fun doing it.'

'So how much do you make?'

'Exactly? I don't know.'

'Come on, you don't keep a record?'

'No. I don't need to keep a record – I know.'

If such a statement came from other sources, it could be immediately filed in a folder labelled 'Bullshit'. But not this one. Almost casually, he mentions that he also bets for other people. That means they give him their money to do their betting for them. It's like he's their investment manager. Since the undoubted buzz that comes from placing a bet is not part of the equation, the only conclusion to come to is that these clients are betting that Virg's instincts are profitable. That's a bottom line credential that's hard to argue with.

He also knows the kind of races you should be playing in and those that should be avoided like the plague.

'I like betting in maidens. There might be thirty in the race but only three or four can win. I know it can be hard to get on each way but if you think it's impossible for one to be out of the frame, I love betting each way at 3–1 or better. All you have to do is listen for what's fancied, have a look at them, and then back up your own opinion. If you don't have your opinion, what's the point of any of it? I like betting three-year-olds in handicaps too. But you'll find that the better races, like in Listed and up, are where the form stands up.'

Most of Virg's betting is done on Irish racing but his contacts stretch across to Britain and he will often bet blind on what he is being told by his pals. 'I know jockeys are terrible tipsters but one or two really know what they're on about. You've just got to know them.'

He has his blindspots, though, just like any punter in a betting shop. He won't go near a horse trained by Dermot Weld or Ger Lyons, and isn't crazy about backing John Oxx's either. Declan McDonogh is his jockey: gives everything a ride and is an animal in a finish. Pat Smullen he likes on the big tracks but not on the small country gaffs. But even going racing every day, and knowing more about form than most of us will ever want to know, isn't enough to stop him falling into the same traps as the rest of us. Mention of a certain horse provokes a noticeable intake of breath.

'Jesus, Regalline: what a bitch. I don't know if she's got a physical problem, or if the problem is in her head, or if she doesn't have a trip,' he says. 'But I've seen her work. It's unbelievable what she does at home. But she won't do it when it matters, a real morning glory. What she probably needs is six furlongs, jump her out and go like fuck. But Kevin doesn't like his horses to lead.'

Illogically, it feels a lot better knowing that Virg was caught by Regalline too. If a pro can get dazzled by a reputation, then it can happen to anyone. He's also dead right about the importance of having faith in your own opinion. It has to be as informed an opinion as you can make it. Then, at the very least, there will be no one else to blame. And, financially, he's hardly playing in a different league. Five hundred is pretty much his maximum, and it's obviously paying off for him. A mention of his name to a couple of the press-room guys who work in the ring results in a narrowing of the eyes and a little nod that is racing's universal acknowledgement for someone worthwhile.

The worrying part is his belief that, without information, betting is little more than just a shot in the dark. I hear stuff, but it's only the faint squeak of a faraway fieldmouse compared to the wall of sound blasting into Virg's ear. There's also his insistence on being at the track every day. He can manage it because there are no other demands on his time. As he says, it beats the hell out of nine-to-five. Virg is playing in a different league, a professional league, and one that chews up and spits out enthusiastic amateurs who have to earn a living in something approximating the real world.

'How's it going for you so far?' he asks.

'Oh, you know, up and down.'

'Which is it? Are you up or down?'

'Slightly up,' I reply, just about truthfully.

'That's good. You can get cracking now. Everything has nearly had a run. The summer's coming. Now's the time to kick on.'

'I suppose so.'

'Want some advice?'

'Always.'

'If you're not sure, stick to what you know.'

'What do you mean?'

'What part of the game do you like most? Handicaps? Sprints? Maidens?'

'I suppose it would be the good stuff. Group races, Listed, the better horses.'

'OK, then, stick with what you know, and the form does work out better in those races.'

'Fair enough, thanks.'

'And give us a shout. Let us know how you're doing. I might be able to help out.'

Running total: + €21.50

Nuking Dougie

21 May 2007

The 'Big L' is turning. Not in any Baryshnikov-like pirouette it has to be said. It's more Brandoesque than that. But the signs are unmistakable, including the most important one of all: a winner! Septimus returns from almost a year off to win the Mooresbridge Stakes at the Curragh. His starting price is 4–1, but €100 at 9–2 is not a problem. In normal circumstances during the race, there wouldn't be a worry – even the hot favourite, Mustameet, helps out by developing a runny nose – but these are not normal circumstances. Septimus is pulling up by the time my brain finally acknowledges that it might be quite a good idea to take a breath.

Maybe it's oxygen deprivation but I've no immediate

desire to take a Dettori-like gallop in front of the stands. This might have something to do with having recently saved my pimply white ass from the financial grinder through ridiculous good fortune. But even while walking towards the post-race press huddle, there is also no denying the rather large dollop of self-satisfaction that Septimus has just injected into my system. He might be the first significant winner in almost twenty goes but there is nobody more smug than the person just shorn of his virginity.

That losing feeling returns, however, when All My Loving is beaten at Chester but, the day after, Pacolet wins at Clonmel and pays almost 4–1 on Betfair. It's enough for the faint Sinatra-like strut that greeted Septimus to briefly transform into a full-on Bee Gee swagger. Family Focus then threatens a beano for much of the straight at Killarney but, ultimately, fails to get past Gentleman Jeff. With €63.66 matched at 8.6 and €36.34 at 9.2, it would have been one helluva result.

The same helpful source that provided Family Focus suggests another Tommy Stack-trained horse the following day. Apparently, Cochlear is a good-thing for the mile maiden. He gets backed to win at €700 and it's smug time again until the halfway mark. The jockey, Wayne Lordan, is sitting pretty waiting to pounce. Everyone else is starting to row like Steve Redgrave trying to stop himself tipping over Niagara Falls, but then Cochlear loses his balance and shambles around at the furlong pole as if he is about to tip over into one of the nearby lakes.

That's another €200 gone, and I lose more on Diamond Necklace at Naas. The obvious thing to do with her is to keep running in maidens but, instead, O'Brien is persevering in better class. A third placing in a Listed race at Gowran proves there is definite ability lurking inside that snootily bred grey frame, and since O'Brien is willing to try her in Group 3 class, who's going to disagree with him? Despite being at Naas to watch the Blue Wind Stakes, the odds on the exchange are much better than in the ring. €100 stands to win €1,150. However, Diamond Necklace never threatens and is well stuffed behind Four Sins. She is starting to provoke some ire: there's something about the way that grey head starts to reach for the sky when the pressure comes on which screams 'jade'.

But even being pick-pocketed by a high-class tramp can't alter the sense of having turned a corner. It's not just because of a couple of winners either. There are little things that mean almost as much. Like in a Monday-evening maiden at Roscommon where In A Rush looks a shoo-in. Dermot Weld's filly was a beaten odds-on shot at Killarney but looks like one to improve for an extra quarter mile and doesn't appear to have much to beat. On the exchanges, she never moves over 6–4. €200 is the least she deserves – talking to Virg has dismissed the concept of points as delusional. With just a couple left to load into the stalls and the bet – €200 at 2–5 – lined up, I press the Submit button. Up comes a notice advising the customer to log in – how moronic must you be to forget something so fundamental. The gates open, which provokes a stream of invective that has the family discreetly vanishing into the kitchen. Except In A Rush finishes only fourth – runs like a dog, in fact. A couple of weeks ago, I know in my water that she would have dotted up.

That may be irrational, but anyone who bets the ponies will never be arrogant enough to dismiss luck as some intangible juju for the weak-minded. There's too much potential for disaster to allow such smug certitude. It's just that luck has had a bad press. Ever since the South African golfer Gary Player bleated on about the harder he worked, the luckier he got, many would rather confess to a case of the galloping clap than admit to events conspiring against them. Instead of the sane acknowledgement that all of us have the significance of ants in the greater scheme of things, we now have control freaks whining on about failure to prepare and all the rest of it. If it really is the case that shallow men believe in luck while strong men believe in cause and effect, then this game would reward those who approach it with a slavish, Boxer-like willingness to work even harder. But it doesn't.

In A Rush aside, the exchanges are becoming less of a challenge. Examples of laying the Montreal Masturbators to lose to the Florida Foreskins are down to only one a week. Despite a broadband connection that's no more broad than Kylie Minogue's backside, it is ridiculously easy to get your money down – on anything. If there is a kid throwing a rock at a coconut in Madagascar right now, there is a good chance you will be able to bet on it, and, thanks to Rupert Murdoch, get instant replays on your TV. Opportunities are endless but a lot of us remain at caveman level.

It's still hard to leave the mindset of simply fancying a horse, reckoning what price is acceptable to back it and then getting the money down. But the real experts can play the computer for every possible edge.

Successfully betting in running, for instance, requires an encyclopaedic knowledge of the horses' running styles, a faster internet connection than Bill Gates' and the finger speed of

Rubinstein on a keyboard. To use two famous jump horses as an example, if you know that Brave Inca will be under pressure from halfway, but will keep finding more for it, then you play the exchanges to find someone who thinks Brave Inca is beaten and is offering extravagant odds as a result. The other extreme also works. Brave Inca's old rival Harchibald always travels through his races with an ease that suggests he will pass the opposition without breaking sweat. However, if you know that, in the past, Harchibald has exhibited an appetite for battle that makes Frankie Howerd look like Otto Skorzeny, then you can keep offering the best odds up to the run-in and hope that Harchie, once again, turns his handsome nose up at the idea of a scrap. To do that, you have to be confident enough – and proficient enough – to ride those digital rails without dithering.

In fact, the sole visit I've made to Betfair's wild side so far is a trip to the pink column for a first stab at playing bookie. On the same evening that Diamond Necklace fails to win any affection, the danger of spurning a Ballydoyle female is brought home with a vengeance. Peeping Fawn has yet to win a race too but, instead of anything psychological being behind that, the evidence of three runs at a mile suggests she simply needs a longer trip. Yet here she is in another mile maiden. Every scintilla of what we've seen says this is too short. At the Curragh and at Gowran, Peeping Fawn has finished like a train. Surely the same will be the case now? But, of course, it isn't.

A tentative offer to risk losses of €200 at 2.1 (just over even money) is gobbled up just before off time. Peeping Fawn's starting price ends up 9–10. She travels well to the straight where her jockey starts to turn the screw. If she really needs a mile-and-a-quarter, then here is where something with more speed should get past her. But nothing does. Instead Peeping Fawn keeps lengthening her stride and is well clear at the line. A final desperate hope that the process might have broken down disappears with a look at the My Account box. Two hundred more has vanished down the information super-drain before Peeping Fawn even appears in the winner's enclosure.

But the beneficial impact of a couple of winners means it can be shrugged off. Not in any Noel Gallagher, couldn't-be-arsed-anyway manner it has to be said. €200 is still €200 and this new Bee Gee vibe won't survive the loss of too many more of them. The most important thing though is that my appetite is back. There were a couple of weeks when even looking at a race was close to becoming a chore and what's the point of carefully avoiding a useful and productive working life if there isn't any fun in it?

This renewed vigour is tested back at Leopardstown on Derrinstown Derby Trial day. Epsom is just three weeks away and today's big race is possibly the most significant warm-up. For three years running at the start of the decade, the winner here was the winner at Epsom. Dylan Thomas won last season, Yeats a couple of seasons before that. If there is a Derby horse in Ireland, it runs here. This time round though, a gallop at Ballydoyle might do just as well. Aidan O'Brien has four of the five runners. Mores Wells is the odd-one-out and also looks one to oppose – he's had his day in the sun. Evidence keeps mounting that most of the Ballydoyle horses are improving by at least half-a-stone for their first runs of the season. Just an hour before the Trial, that theory is backed up by Astronomer Royal winning the French 2,000 Guineas in Longchamp. This is going to be an O'Brien gig. The question is, which one? The answer is tantalising enough to have everybody's antennae up and whirring.

The weigh room is the nerve centre of every racecourse, and always holds a particular fascination for those who can't get in. Normally, being prevented from entering anywhere is enough to turn your average Irish racegoer into a commando but, whereas most 'reserved' areas are an aspirational concept, the weigh room is different in that someone in a white coat occasionally asks people for ID. Not unnaturally then, for a relatively small room populated almost exclusively by trainers, jockeys, hacks, bookmakers' representatives and a few determined under-the-wire merchants, there is enough gossip to make Joan Rivers look like Ingmar Bergman. All kinds of information is circulating, mostly third- or fourth-hand with, occasionally, some coveted chunks of second-hand scuttlebuck. It's one of those strange contradictions that much of the horsey population spends its time furtively trying to get an edge on the world and yet they are unable to keep their mouths shut. For a race like the Derrinstown Derby Trial, however, with everything concentrated into one yard, there is a reassuring consistency about the signals.

Macarthur is being backed with the same sort of certainty Dougie had about nuking the hell out of the Chinese in Korea. He may have ground to make up on Mores Wells from last month but, pretty soon, he is odds-on and getting shorter all the time. There is no doubt that Macarthur is 'the one' from Ballydoyle. Even before the race starts, his odds shorten for Epsom. This is going to be a coronation. However, by pressing an ear closer to the grapevine, it emerges that things may not be quite so straightforward. Mac may be 'the one' for most of those close to Ballydoyle but another trainer discloses that, a few months ago, Aidan had revealed it was Archipenko whom he figured might turn into a Derby winner. Archipenko, however, is having his first start of the year and O'Brien has made no secret, in the *Racing Post*, that he believes the colt is only just ready for a run and will be the better for it. He also reports that Macarthur has had some muscle trouble since his last race.

As the off-time looms, Mac is a heavy odds-on favourite. It doesn't seem to matter to anyone else at Leopardstown, but betting so tight on a horse with some tweaky muscles doesn't seem the brightest strategy in the world. So, by taking the view that the favourite is vulnerable, that Archipenko is here just to blow the cobwebs off, and that Hernando Cortes couldn't even manage to blow a cobweb away, I'm left with Yellowstone, who just happens to be 16–1 on Betfair and only 10–1 with the bookies. This is the kind of edge the exchanges sometimes throw up. It's one worth waiting for. This will be Yellowstone's third start of the year so he is a tight-fit. He didn't run badly in the 2,000 Guineas at Newmarket when he was drawn on the wrong side and, on breeding, this trip shouldn't be a problem. With doubts about everything else, he's the only logical bet at the odds. By the time, 17–1 appears on screen for €100, it is obvious there is only one clear-thinking bet. And that's where the Gary Players of this world fall down: because Yellowstone doesn't win. He should win, but he doesn't. No matter how po-faced the approach is, there is still too much out of our control. Like, for instance, the jockey.

It's not Johnny Murtagh's finest moment. He has Yellowstone alongside Archipenko at the back of the field but, when Mick Kinane secures a run up the inside, Murtagh appears to hesitate for a moment before launching his own challenge on the outside. Yellowstone closes but is still three-quarters-of-a-length down at the line. That brief hesitation costs big time. It's just a second, but it's enough. Riding on the flat is all about timing. In the vast majority of cases, a horse has one kick in him, and where the likes of Kinane and Murtagh earn their corn is by knowing when best to use it. Go too soon and you risk being mown down before the line. Go too late and you get a Yellowstone. The pressure comes from having to make these judgements in milliseconds.

As a jockey capable of real inspiration, Murtagh can throw in his fair share of ordinary rides. Streaky is a word sometimes used for him. It's hardly surprising really: for a man who has had to endure tortuous weight trouble, it's a wonder Murtagh is still operating to the level he does. Built like a solid welterweight required to make bantamweight, he is physically suited to almost anything else besides keeping his body under eight-stone-ten in order to ride racehorses. However, even making such allowances can't disguise how the cocksure figure is, like most jockeys, prone to the occasional clanger. Mind you, it can't help to have spent his career tangling with Mr Kinane. Where Murtagh is often inspirational, his great rival is always coldly ruthless.

Perhaps the most memorable example of the mental tug-of-war between the two finest riders of their generation came in the 2003 Irish 1,000 Guineas when, with the whole of the Curragh available to his left, Murtagh chose an adventurous route up the inside on the odds-on French champion Six Perfections. Kinane's beady eye read the situation immediately. He delayed his own run to keep the favourite trapped and held her there long enough to allow his filly to fall across the line in front. He got lots of kudos for that but, a year before, in a minor three-horse race at Listowel, there was maybe an even greater example of the psychological battles that can turn the most nondescript contests into fascinating daily mini-dramas.

Faced with Murtagh on a 2–5 favourite called Millstreet, Kinane decided to make the running on a horse called Sorcerous. Everything was as expected, until the turn into the straight which contains a dog-leg halfway up it. Kinane eased off the rail slightly, enough to create an opening. There wasn't much room but, watching the race, it seemed like we could hear his brain calculating how much would be needed to tempt the man behind him. Millstreet was going so well, all he needed was a switch to the outside and he would win comfortably. But Kinane kept inviting. For a split second there was enough room for Murtagh to get up. The decision to win in routine fashion or with a touch of flamboyance had to be taken in a moment and Murtagh couldn't resist the temptation. Sure enough, as soon as Millstreet's nose appeared at Sorcerous' flank, Kinane drifted back in. His rival snatched up and switched to the outside. But it was too late. Kinane came back looking grave as ever. Murtagh had the ashen look of someone who'd just been mugged.

Right now, I know how he felt.

Running total: + €341.50

Frankie s Deep-Throat Potion

4 June

Slagging off jockeys is the easiest exercise in racing. It's fun too – which is just as well, since there isn't a race fan alive who hasn't, at some stage of their lives, felt they've done their dough as a result of some overwhelming piece of stupidity by a little man in fancy dress. So, when it happens, sometimes there's nothing else left but to curse their miniature, black souls to hell.

Everyone's different though. Many manage to swallow their bile and maybe find a large wall to silently batter their brains against after being subjected to what is euphemistically called 'pilot error'. However, only occasionally does a jockey have to put up with actual abuse. There have been displays of gross ineptitude on racecourses in Ireland, which in more excitable territories, would have had the locals reaching for petrol bombs. But here there's almost a protocol: there might be a shout or two from the punters but, in return, the jockey will exhibit the kind of skin that is so thick, it normally only exists around the nether regions of veteran Mongol goatherders. Their composure can be attributed to the fact that any jockey with a functioning brain cell, and admittedly there are those who doubt such creatures exist, knows that they're the ones living the dream.

That absolute certainty is unavoidable when you come to Epsom for the Derby, still the greatest day of the racing year. Recently, it has become fashionable to proclaim how unfashionable a mile-and-a-half around a glorified fairground ride is for some of the best horses in the world. But, somehow, that still doesn't stop everyone wanting to win it.

This is Derby number 228 and, more than anything, it's the history of this race that has defined the industry. From the breeding side, to racing the greatest champions, to providing a centrepiece of excellence around which all else hangs, the Derby defines every year. Plenty of people automatically associate a year with its Derby winner. 1968 may have been the summer of riots but, much more important, was Sir Ivor and Piggott bolting up. The Berlin Wall might have come down in 1989, but mention the year to many of the 100,000 people attending this year's Derby and it's Nashwan and Willie Carson they'll throw back at you, not Gorbachev.

It's always the horse and jockey that conjure the lasting image. All the stress might sit on the trainer's shoulders and the owner may be the one coughing up all the money, but no youngster ever rode a bike down a hill pretending they trained or owned this mythical champion underneath them. The thrill is in being on board.

Through reasons of talent, aptitude – and let's not fool ourselves – size, not everyone gets the chance to live the dream of whistling around Tattenham Corner on Nijinsky. But at the back of our heads remains the flame that ignited the passion for the game in the first place. So, when the eighteen runners and riders parade in front of the stands, and Messrs Dettori, Kinane & Co. look up at the packed stands, they're looking at a lot of extremely jealous people. Even the Queen must wonder how she would go about riding the hot favourite Authorized.

Today, practically every jockey in the western hemisphere appears to be riding for Aidan O'Brien. Eight of the runners are from Ballydoyle, a record total from one source, and as clear a sign as anyone needs that so many darts are being thrown at the board only in the fervent hope that one might stick. It's a rule as old as the Derby: if a trainer thinks he has a hatful up to classic standard, then he doesn't have anything. By common consent, it is Peter Chapple Hyam who has the outstanding mile-and-a-half three-year-old this year in Authorized, who must not only carry Frankie Dettori, but also the colossal media bandwagon that accompanies the little Italian.

Dettori is an acquired taste. For every ten who love his ebullience and that ridiculous accent, there is sure to be someone else who will dismiss him as a loud fake. A couple of short interviews are no basis for any sort of conclusive verdict but the fake tag does seem to be way off beam. Prolonged exposure to all that Who's-the-Daddy? stuff would have most of us eventually reaching for a revolver, but that's just Frankie. He is what he is and we should be grateful, since he is the face of the game to the wider public in these islands. Never ever forget that John McCririck is next in line.

Today, Frankie is the only story in town and, after fourteen losers in the race, he wants to win more than any other, it's hardly a surprise that the Derby is being billed as the Frankie show. There is an almost-perceptible wave of goodwill pulling him towards the finishing line. From a betting point of view, however, it's probably best to do ice-cold right now rather than gooey feel-good.

So, boiling it down, this Derby can only have two results. Either Authorized will hose up or there'll be a shock result. A battling neck success by the favourite doesn't even feature on the radar. That's just a hunch, but a reasonable one. There's little doubt that he is impossible to crab on form and preparation, but the same was said of the last three odds-on favourites and they all got stuffed. Nevertheless, the idea of hanging out for evens somewhere and going for broke with the whole kit-and-caboodle is tempting. In fact it is far too tempting, and it's born out of an impulse that, at this stage in the project really should be better behaved. Eventually, sanity gets a muzzle on its dark cousin but, sad to say, not deciding on an Authorized blowout is probably due more to prejudice than any good sense.

Confidence is always described as being the key weapon in a jockey's armoury but it always seems that Dettori is more reliant on it than most. At his bubbly best, there's no one better, and because he has such style in the saddle, he can do things that make people shake their heads and smile at the sheer skill of it all. But when the bubbles disappear, it can be a flatter story than the final *Star Wars*. It's a decade since the biggest cock-up of Frankie's career but the thought still won't go away that, with all this pressure, all that Mediterranean emotion might erupt into a brainstorm of tropical intensity.

The impression left when Swain lost his chance of winning the Breeders' Cup Classic remains vivid – and with Frankie more than anyone. He has already said that if there's ever a *This Is Your Life* on him, Swain will probably come clumping on just to remind everyone of that horror show. Basically, he lost it. After doing the hard job of smuggling the European turf champion into a position to beat the best Yanks on dirt, he started slapping Swain's arse as if it was some particularly dusty carpet – except he got to work with his left hand. Not unnaturally, Swain reacted to this assault by drifting right to such an extent that he ended up almost mowing down the photographers in position under the stands. Frankie's initial pop-eyed response was to blame said snappers for distracting Swain. He fooled no one. Dettori's record since has firmly put to bed any suggestion that he is one of those sportsmen who never fails to rise to the small occasion, but the nagging doubt remains. He's coming here on a Derby losing streak and a worryingly long losing stretch in the past fortnight. Godolphin, his main employers, are also colder than Christmas when it comes to winning form. There's no point ignoring the little voice that keeps saying another psychological eruption wouldn't be the weirdest thing to ever happen.

Plus, it's not as if shock candidates have to be tortuously dug out of the formbook. Who'd have thought a couple of months ago at Leopardstown that Mahler would end up making the Derby? But here he is, and alongside is Yellowstone. Archipenko is second-favourite and yet the horse that should have beaten him in the Trial is gliding between 70–1 and 80–1 on Betfair. It's a no-brainer, each way bet, although there is also no getting away from the fact that place betting on the exchanges can often be lousy value.

Mahler is a different beast. He, too, was trading at huge odds on Betfair last night but the idea of losing out on even better prices today prevented me from playing. Greed got its just desserts and, lo and behold, 'Pricewise' in the *Racing Post* tips him up at 50–1 and Mahler's odds start dropping fast. The resulting fury I feel at having missed out on the real big stuff is diluted by a ridiculous sense of proprietorial pride. That's my boy, Gustav, you underappreciated genius, you. The result is that his odds plummet to 20–1 and 33–1 is the best offer on the exchange. The upside comes from being at least on the same sort of wavelength as the column that labels itself the world's best tipping service. We are communal beasts after all – only the psychotic get off on being different all the time.

The race itself isn't so much a race as a coronation. Yellowstone starts at the back and stays there while Mahler suffers another attack of the slows. At the top of the hill, he gets a brief glimpse of reflected fame as he races alongside Authorized. But it is very brief.

Another €200 is gone. But it doesn't matter.

It should matter, and it does in an annoying, scab-on-the-elbow kind of way but not enough to deflect from one of the most impressive Derby winners you'll ever see. Authorized cruises around the hurdy-gurdy excuse for a racetrack like he's on rails. The newspaper game can place enough time pressure to make anyone reach for the most convenient cliché but if poetry in motion ever meant anything, it was surely for something like this. For those of us who think a galloping thoroughbred is a thing of beauty, it's a rare treat to watch this magnificent bay colt pass the post with his tongue lolling out in contempt of the opposition behind him. Authorized really does look that good. If anyone needs a bet to get a kick out of him today, then they should rent a spot in their local casino and simply pump the slots.

Not surprisingly, the story is Frankie. But, even while writing it up, there are those in the long media room at the top of the Queen's Stand who pepper the quietly frantic atmosphere with suggestions that a rare horse is being overlooked because of the public's demand for Dettori. Maybe there's something in it but to dismiss the ride because he was on the best horse is to be horribly negative about a wonderfully ballsy effort. The early pace up that hill was enough to have the field stretched after a couple of furlongs and the easy option on a hot favourite would have been to sit close off it and appear to give the horse every chance. For a jockey low on winners and high on the pressure of an entire industry willing him to succeed, the temptation to try and stay out of trouble must have been huge. Instead, Frankie backed his instincts, took his time and collected. All it needs to be perfect is for someone else to be collecting a large cheque.

€5,000 to €4,000 has a nice ring to it. Who knew Authorized would end up odds against? The Frankie Factor might have been ditched this morning in a hurry. No matter what any flint-eyed pro might say, it would have felt better to win big on the Derby winner rather than some 5–4 job in a maiden at Bellewstown. Anyone who doesn't think so may as well be betting on those ridiculous virtual reality races the betting shops put on for the brain dead. Authorized's backers, and one guy is reported to have had a cool half a million on, will always look back on the old clips they play on the telly every year and feel more than a little tremor of nostalgia when Derby 2007 is replayed. They've bought their own little bit of history, whether it's for a fiver or with five zeroes added on.

However, everything is relative. A couple of days later, Naas on a Bank Holiday Monday may not have the lustre of Epsom, but it does have a filly called Potion running in the mile-and-a-quarter fillies handicap.

Potion is no star. The most noteworthy thing about her is that she is owned by J.P. McManus' daughter, Sue Ann. But she did manage to finish runner-up in a Tralee maiden as a two-year-old and her only start this year was in that hot Leopardstown maiden that Karen and her family watched from the traffic jam. There's still even a hazy impression of her black colours going past us, admittedly a long way behind the winner – but seeing as the winner was All My Loving, Friday's Epsom Oaks third, it was hardly a disgrace to get outclassed. A handicap for fillies rated between fifty and eighty is a very different kettle of fish. Potion has to be a player now.

In the parade ring, she looks ready to run for her life, all bounce, but not so much that she's ready to boil away her chance. A chestnut creature called Baby Blue Eyes is the big danger in the betting but, in the looks stakes, Potion is a clear winner. Unfortunately, there's no pay out on beauty. While contemplating the unfairness of such a state of affairs, the importance of actually being present on the racecourse is emphasised in a big way.

As heads-ups go, it's pretty much unbeatable. If the value of a tip can be gauged by the volume at which it is delivered, then this one is whispered gold. Potion, apparently, is ready to run for her life, this is her classic – a now-or-never job. My very own Deep Throat is one of those characters who like to speak with racecards covering their mouths. To hear him I have to press my head closer than I should necessarily have to with another man. But it's a small price to pay. 'DT' knows the night before what each trainer in south Tipperary is going to have for his breakfast.

'They won't see this thing's arse for grass,' he sighs, lips barely moving. 'You can have what you like on, but keep it to yourself.'

Even while digesting this joyful news, there is the nagging question of why 'DT' is telling me. For years, he has been one of those faces that you see at the races and might occasionally nod at in acknowledgement. If we've exchanged more than twenty words, it would be a surprise. The receptionist at the Paddy Power office knows me better. Has he slipped and knocked his head? Is he drunk?

'As I say, keep it to yourself,' he repeats, and walks off, the card still protecting his mouth from running away.

In such a situation – with doubts piling in about why I should be so fortunate – a shrewd man will step back, consider the *qui bono* bit, and come to a rational and sensible conclusion: emulating such behaviour while busily legging it to the ring is difficult. Forget Betfair, this is going to be a real job.

Potion opens at 7–2 and quickly tightens to 100–30. With over five minutes to the off-time, it's tempting to play now and find someplace dark and private to quietly panic. But with €500, the max, moistening in my sweaty paw, something says wait. It's the same sort of greed that saw Mahler's big odds disappear, but, this time, it pays off. Some serious wedge starts appearing for Baby Blue Eyes. Arms begin busily tic-tacking and bookies' runners start pushing past, shouting into walkie-talkies like Secret Service agents with a president down. Potion's price starts to lengthen to 4–1, then 9–2 and then, as the horses start to load, she hits 5–1. Normally, such a drift would be a big worry, but not this time. Then this brave soul goes 11–2.

'Twenty-seven fifty to a monkey,' my benefactor shouts to his clerk. 'Quickly now.'

'DT' and his pals are evidently made of hardier stuff because they leave it even later, but they get enough down for Potion's starting price to be 4–1.

Fran Berry makes full use of stall two and bounces Potion out quickly to take up second position and sit in what's called the 'cat-bird' seat just off the leader's tail. Early in the straight, he pounces and quickly gets the others at it. A furlong out, there's a brief stab of concern when the outsider, Chakeera, threatens to run on, but Potion has three-quarters-of-a-length in hand at the line. As she goes by the post, the Tote Hall is at the eye of only a minor shrieking storm.

Euphoric levitation as a mode of transport has a lot to recommend it, especially when it takes you a good foot off terra firma. There's nothing quite like the rush a big win gives.

As Virgil says, quick money is the best of all. But there's more to it this time. Everything came together. Potion was a standout in the parade ring, and her form gave her a big shout. But then came that information to wrap up the proposition. Who knows why 'DT' bleated? Maybe Virgil has been talking to people. But who cares? She's won.

The €3,000 feels like nothing but that's because of the €500 notes. Without wishing to sound all 'love me, love me, I'm an innocent', the purple money really does have a luxuriant richness to it that's enough to make you feel quite rakish. Maybe that's why it feels so easy to play up one of them in the last race.

Dermot Weld's Profound Beauty is expected to be an odds-on favourite for the fillies maiden over ten furlongs. Earlier in the day, the trainer's son Kris had watched a race on the TV in the press room. Behind his easy-going exterior, Weld Junior is very much a chip off the block when it comes to calculating his chances of winning. He also has the charitable habit of sharing some of those thoughts with some of the press-room inhabitants.

'I suppose you'll win the last, Kris.'

'Ah, she should win, shouldn't she?'

The enquiring tone is purely polite. He doesn't need anyone else to tell him that Profound Beauty is a worthy favourite. But it's good to hear him add nothing else. Nothing about her missing any work recently or that he's worried about the ground. It's just a straightforward statement of the obvious. So, if the Weld team believe she'll win, who's going to argue?

There's even a shade of odds against about her, and €500 will generate €550. It's the same bookie who goes the 11–10.

There's a brief glance and he has to stifle a grin. The sound of money being played up is sweet soul music to most book-makers. I make a point of watching the race from the same place and in front of the same TV. Except that seems a bit too much like voodoo which results in a swift move across the Tote Hall to another screen. But that feels like too much of a point so the race begins with me dithering between two televisions.

The funky two-step is redundant from the start. Pat Smullen gives Profound Beauty a kick in the belly and she makes all the running to win on her own. Afterwards, Weld tells us he thinks she's Group 1 class. Kris stands nearby looking like a cat who has just tucked into a sizeable canary. He deserves to. But there's only one winner in the smug stakes.

No owner has ever been happier in this winner's enclosure. No horse has ever looked better, or more beautiful, or more intelligent than Profound Beauty does right now. As for Potion, well, she deserves a place in the pantheon of greats: right up there alongside Authorized. Maybe they'll end up having foals together. That would be so great, they deserve each other.

'You can't say you weren't told, anyway,' says Kris quietly, as the huddle breaks up.

In return, he gets a smile that feels beatific but probably looks like the gurning of an Easter Island idiot. Who cares? No Derby winner ever left Epsom with more of a bounce in his step than me. Look out Naas, it's Bee-Gee time!

Running total: + €3,250

SpongeBob s Ulster Fry

6 June

If it's true that a woman's instinct for gambling is satisfied by marriage, then her man is probably better off pretending the same. As one prominent Curragh trainer says, when it comes to betting, an ignorant woman is a happy woman. Leaving aside the ethics, one can see his point, and also recognise why such thoughts are usually left unexpressed until he is sure there is at least fifty miles of clear ground between him and Mrs Trainer.

Betting is a take-it-or-leave-it bit of fun for most of the wiser sex. Only the briefest glance into a betting shop will reveal it to be an overwhelmingly male domain. Even today, there are many women who still regard a visit to a bookies with only slightly less distaste than they would a trip to Chubby Brown's underpants.

At the races themselves, it's a similar story. During festivals especially, younger female souls might breach the gender divide and trawl the betting ring, but such appearances are not always appreciated by bookmakers who tend to complain bitterly about having to take €2 each way bets on odds-on favourites. Such sexist condescension usually results in 'the laydeez' being steered towards the Tote, where the queuing is no doubt made slightly less unbearable by discussing why on earth 'the lads' get so serious about it all.

What 'the laydeez' fail to get is that betting the ponies is not just about money. The pay-off is actually just an expression of something much more fundamental, something rooted in male DNA. In the schoolyard, there can hardly ever have been a race, fight or taunt, where the competitive flames weren't fanned by a sneering invitation of 'wanna bet?' We might be bigger and older now, but the world is still inviting us to back ourselves.

As a result, placing a bet is not so much another school-yard pissing contest as a very personal way of validating your own judgement. Getting it right can actually be a helluva lot more important than how much you get.

The greatest compliment any punter can receive is to be regarded as a 'good judge'. Men have had their lives vindi-cated by those two words. Virgil, for instance, and 'DT' are good judges, their opinions are sought-after. They are people of substance. Such a reputation matters to them, possibly more than they will ever admit – after all, they have devoted much of their lives to securing it.

And a fundamental test for this 'good judge' status is to ask yourself if you bet because you can afford to or because you can't afford not to. Honestly facing up to this question is something that defeats a lot of us wannabes.

Right now, on the back of Potion and Profound Beauty, it's possible – just – to believe that this little project is on the up and up. But the more calculating among you will have established that we are a quarter of the way through the season and there's still the little matter of almost €42,000 to come up with. And no matter how hard that Bee-Gee smugness is incubated, it can't disguise the fact that I'm not getting it right nearly often enough to qualify for the can't-afford-not-to category.

Divide the season up into months and an average of over €6,000 profit is needed in each one of them. That means I need a couple of Potion days each month as well as keeping losses to a minimum. No brief injection of happy-happy adrenalin can disguise the increasing doubts that such a target may be way too ambitious. Right now, my judgement isn't completely shrivelled, not yet anyway, but neither is it in any danger of taking a bookmaker's eye out.

It's hard to get away from the reality that the one horse I've laid to lose on Betfair so far is Peeping Fawn and she dotted up, but that's only a fraction of the story. Not only did Peeping Fawn win, eleven days later she ran in the 1,000 Guineas at the Curragh and managed to finish third. Just five days after that, she appeared again and was unlucky not to win the Epsom Oaks. Add all that up and you have the hard and unyielding truth that this hot, pro-punter decided one of the best classic fillies in Europe hadn't a hope of winning a midweek maiden at Naas. It takes a special kind of genius to do that.

It also requires a unique level of skill to realise that both

Cockney Rebel and Finsceal Beo are absolute good-things for the Irish Guineas races and not back either. In the filly's case, there is at least the argument that she was a red-hot favourite and, at 9–10 odds, squeezing home by a neck from a 66–1 shot is not particularly beneficial to anyone's coronary status. But there's no excuse at all for Cockney Rebel. Here was a Newmarket Guineas winner who, if he was trained by a big name, would be a 4–6 favourite to complete the double. But there was 7–4 available on the track and over 2–1 on the exchanges: which is some kind of insult to Geoff Huffer, when you think about it. He may not be one of the bigwigs training in Newmarket but he's no Group 1 virgin, and he has never made any secret of believing that Cockney Rebel is by far the best he has ever had. Mind you, for someone who has done jail-time for evading duty payments, there are insults and then there are insults.

In order to turn things round, I concede that some changes are going to have to be made and a fundamental one is that going to the races more often must be a priority. It's no coincidence that my best day so far happened as a result of hanging around a parade ring. No amount of staring at a computer would have encouraged a €500 bet on a relatively nondescript mare in a mundane handicap. Virgil & Co. insist on going to every dogsbody of a meeting in the country, even when there are only three flat races on a wet Wednesday evening in Downpatrick. They're not doing that because of a love of the open road.

However, they have a huge advantage by at least being in a position to do so. If there's one thing worth putting money on, it is that the vast majority of the guys who are making a living through punting are single. No man with a significant other can live the kind of lifestyle where Downpatrick on a Wednesday is followed by Limerick on a Thursday and then on to Wexford the following day. Through the summer and into autumn, the schedule is relentless. Cars become second homes, merging with their owners in an osmotic fervour to rival that of Flann O'Brien and his policeman's bike.

For young men, there is a certain appeal in this – for a while. Some even continue to believe they're living some wildly exciting rock 'n' roll existence, although having to spend an overnight in Ballinrobe is rather more Daniel O'Donnell than Mick Jagger. A much younger version of me did about a year-and-a-half on the racing roller-coaster, working for an agency and going to all the gaff meetings that the papers wouldn't send their own hacks to. It was hectic and monotonous, different and yet mind-warpingly repetitive. There's nothing quite like having to supply different papers with different reports on the same stuff, and all against the clock. There are worse things, of course, but nothing quite the same. And this was in the prehistoric days of phoning in copy to the newspaper. On one memorable occasion, a personal best was set in Down Royal when thirteen reports had to be 'shouted'. The lights were being turned off as the last report was hoarsely delivered to the *Sunday Whine* or whatever in nearby Belfast. The copy-taker was so bored with the material, she started getting frisky. 'Ye've a lovely voice, love,' she breathed. 'Fancy an Ulster frrryyy – for breakfast?'

But it's simply not possible to keep running on that sort of summer treadmill if there is someone at home and if kids come along, it's goodnight Kilbeggan. As it is, there's unholy war just to get to see a race on TV. There's nothing like a couple of children in whinge mode to distract you from concentrating on the 6.20 from Clonmel. After a while, the easy option is to simply give up when switching to the racing channel causes apoplexy in a bolshy three-year-old with a serious devotion to SpongeBob SquarePants. The result is a slightly less than comprehensive knowledge of form, but what I can tell you is that all that speculation about SpongeBob being gay is spectacularly off the mark as it's clearly Squidward who could light the flame at the Pink Olympics. A longheld desire to keep the television-count of our house down to just one has to be done away with and, even then, it will be a struggle to keep on top of things.

There's also going to have to be a major testosterone injection when it comes to actually getting the money down. Every 'how to' book ever written stresses the need for discipline and not losing the run of yourself, but there's actually a danger in going too far down that road. There have been times when the idea of getting some serious dosh down had produced a jumpiness that only George Bush driving through downtown Fallujah in an open-top might recognise. For someone who started off afraid about reckless impulse taking over, this is something of a worry.

The legendary English journalist, Richard Baerlein, wrote after watching Shergar win his first classic trial that it was time to bet like men. Likewise here, it's time I started betting like I'm in possession of a pair. No more sneaky €30 and €50 bets on long shots. If they really have a chance, then I need to get some serious stuff down. The idea alone will be enough to find out if it's a genuine fancy or just a hunch.

What's really needed though is a spectacular – something to make those sober ideas of a €500 maximum redundant. Make it a double-figure price and who knows how much might go on. It can happen. The memory of Black Minnaloushe winning the Irish Guineas in 2001 is still enough to rouse a tremble from that semi-dormant judgement muscle. Beaten in his first couple of starts in Ireland that year, Black Minnaloushe also ran in the French Guineas where he was brought with a run so wide that it looked like he wanted to stop off at the Bois de Boulogne for *un café et une balle de foin*. Finishing that far back meant, however, that he was an unconsidered 33–1 shot for his return to the Curragh. In the event, he ended up doubled with the 20–1 Imagine which, by some miracle, came off for the sum total of a fiver. Right now, in similar circumstances, it's nice to think some serious business would be done at those odds.

But there's no point waiting. Girding the financial loin also means having to use it more. Betting for the sake of it is stupid, but the volume of bets does have to pick up. If the professionals in the ring are willing to wade in two or three times a day, then it is obviously important. The problem is that you can do that more confidently when you're in the middle of the action rather than stuck at home fighting with SpongeBob for the remote. There's no getting away from it: the Sponge is going to have to get taken out.

He gets a temporary reprieve, however, as work requires a trip to Tipperary. The return of racing's most controversial figure demands nothing less.

Running total: + €3,050

The Fallon Idol

7 June

Is Kieren Fallon colour blind? It's worth asking because it might help the guy if he is. Looking back in black and white could make it easier to cope with everyone else's determination to stare at him the same way. Entering the world of racing's most notorious jockey must sometimes feel like leaving a colour photograph and stepping into its negative – no shades allowed.

This evening at Tipperary, the man who polarises opinion like no one else is returning to race-riding after a six-month ban for cocaine use. He is also in the middle of a High Court appeal in London to get corruption charges against him dropped. The trial, into allegations of defrauding Betfair customers by passing on information to people who lay horses to lose, is scheduled for late September. Not unnaturally, Fallon would rather not have to face any trial. Having the charges dropped would also give him the chance to ride in the UK again – something he has been banned from doing since July 2006 – and repay the loyalty of John Magnier & Co. at Coolmore for whom he is first jockey.

When Fallon's defenders complain about media hype revolving around their man, it's as futile as complaining about water flowing downhill. In an age when Z-list celebrities can make a living out of their own cartoon personalities, consider the ingredients of the previous paragraph and then try to argue that anyone with even the slightest interest in the game isn't entitled to be transfixed. It's the biggest racing story for decades.

Certainly no one but Fallon could assemble such a media presence at a midweek meeting that normally wouldn't rate more than a couple of paragraphs. The tiny press room struggles to cope at the best of times. This evening, it's swamped like a fart in a hurricane. As well as domestic fly-by-nights, there's also a contingent from Britain for whom Fallon has always been like cat-nip. Throw in a phalanx of photographers and we're bouncing around like a free-for-all at Clapham Junction. Mercifully, the overspill is escorted by the racecourse manager to a part of the bar in the stand where he pulls out all the stops to get us powered up.

'There are about 800 more people here than there was last year,' he informs us.

It's a good bet that most of them are wielding either laptops or cameras. In the hack pack generally, as everywhere else, there are deeply entrenched views of the man we are all here to gawp at. One English journo swears he starts to itch when he even hears Fallon's name mentioned, and there's no getting away from the fact that some of the jockey's reported exploits over the years can seem more than a little seedy. Others, however, have scribbled such slavering adulation that you sometimes feel like closing the door in order to let nature take its course. As always, the reality is probably altogether more mundane. But there is one thing that the six-times champion definitely does not do, and that is any shade of grey.

The man himself arrives an hour before the first race, slips into the weigh room and comes out for his first ride back with a tiny touch of drama. The five other jockeys are almost at the parade ring, a couple of hundred yards away, before Fallon emerges. He blazes defiance, chin upturned with eyes determinedly fixed straight ahead: so much so that a youngster requesting an autograph is obliged without Fallon even seeming to look at the proffered racecard. His whole stance is an exaggerated statement designed for a world he knows is scrutinising his every move. It must be an exhausting way to live.

If he's worried about the public reaction, however, he is quickly put right. A spontaneous round of applause welcomes him even before he gets to the parade ring. Among those willing to raise their voices, there's only goodwill. The sceptics choose to remain silent – though the silence is deafening.

There's no denying that constant references to the 'integrity of the sport' can sound incredibly po-faced. After all, this sport is also an industry that generates billions and, when it comes to business, there is only one bottom line.

There are plenty in the game who aren't able to even spell 'ethic' but have the sort of beautiful minds that can calculate the over-round on every race between here and Bangalore in seconds. As a result, only the terminally dull or incredibly naïve can imagine that there isn't a current of roguery pulsing underneath racing's shiny surface.

At the very least, there isn't a jockey alive who can say they haven't, at some stage of their career, given one an easy. In the convoluted decorum of the game, that's not strictly the same as deliberately stopping one from winning. It's a distinction as fine as the pronunciation of tomato, but important none-theless. What is certain is that any young jockey starting out in the sport has to do what they're told by trainers, or else face rapid unemployment. So when a hungry, young rider, eager to get ahead, is told 'not today sunshine', he or she faces a choice: obey, and get on the next day, or sleep with a clear conscience. And integrity is a cold companion when coping with the nightmare of other people winning on your horses.

But it's one thing being an apprentice on the make and quite another to have one of the top jockeys of his generation snarled up in something like this. Most of us rather relish a bit of roguery, especially if we're in on it. But what Fallon is accused of is much more fundamental in that the police believe he is in the middle of a systematic deception of the betting public. Since it's everyone in betting shops through-out these islands who provide racing's basic funding, that is a fundamental threat to the sport's core. Only the gullible believe the game can ever be completely straight, but punters have to know that every effort is being made to keep it as straight as possible.

From an Irish point of view, however, there is the little matter of history when Britain's racing authorities start to clamber up on top of racing's rather shaky morality mountain. When disapprobation for 'one of our own' comes with an English accent, there is a national reflex to start circling the wagons. Osama bin Laden could be accused of being an entirely unreasonable chap by the authorities in London but there remains a sizeable chunk of the wrap-the-green-flag-around-me merchants here who would give the Saudi loon a cuddle if it meant going against what they would see as the establishment grain in England. So much is obvious during Fallon's triumphant march to the ring.

'The Brits are going to love this,' beams one young man, who then gazes at the skyline with an icy stare that suggests he's looking for any low-flying chariots swinging past.

It's not just racegoers either. My own father, a man who knows nothing about horses and cares even less, has had enough of the ravenous coverage of this story seep into his psyche that he has even asked if Fallon is being targeted in Britain because he's Irish. Sadly, there have been times when such suspicion has been justified, but, in this case, it's hardly a runner. If Irish jockeys in England were being discriminated against because of their nationality, there would hardly be any jockeys at all. A quick look at the rider's championship table reveals that seven of the top ten are as Irish as white pudding. The national thing doesn't really fit.

But whether you think Fallon is sinner or saint, there does seem to be general agreement on this side of the Irish Sea that banning him from riding in the UK while he awaits trial sends the innocent-until-proven-guilty theory scurrying out the window. It's a dramatic step that has steered the Horse Racing Authority and the City of London police into a corner that they didn't have to go near but which means they now have to secure their result or forget about any concept of credibility for a generation. The worrying part for them is that what evidence they appear to have looks about as tight as a Temperance meeting.

It all comes down to Virgil's favourite word, information, and how you distinguish it from other words, such as gossip. Fallon and two other jockeys, Fergal Lynch and Darren Williams, are accused of passing on information to punters who then used it to bet and lay horses on Betfair. The police obviously think they have enough to prove the jockeys got kickbacks for their tips. Fallon vehemently argues he didn't know who he was talking to and was simply chatting about racing as he would with anyone. Even allowing for most punters' instinct to believe the worst, it's not impossible to see what he means.

Jockeys, despite the fact they are almost always rubbish tipsters, spend a good part of their lives getting asked the question that anyone with even the mildest connection with the sport learns to loathe, 'Any tips?' People whose judgement is clearly bad enough to make them a danger to themselves have even been known to ask newspaper reporters for tips. On a racecourse, the phrase 'heard anything?' is as natural a greeting as 'hello'. It's simply the basic element in the oxygen of rumour that keeps every race meeting breathing. Any jockey capable of putting a leg either side of a horse is invariably going to get asked his opinion. How you are supposed to distinguish between fobbing someone off with an idle declaration that they should win the first and something more sinister is a linguistic puzzle that would have Wittgenstein scratching his head. It's also part of a story that will dominate this entire season.

Such considerations are on hold, however, as Fallon's first ride, The Bogberry, overcomes trouble in running to win. The jockey returns to thunderous applause and is swarmed by the hack pack. He looks at us with all the relish that a fat man reserves for an especially steep hill. But he's game enough and immediately allows himself to become a five-foot three-inch, eight-and-a-half-stone eye to a considerably weighty storm.

Fallon's a curious character, even without all the baggage he has to carry around. It has to be said that any one-to-one contact I've had with him has been mostly restricted to phone interviews and nods of acknowledgement at the races. But for someone who has found himself in the media spotlight more often than anyone would like, he remains disarmingly open if he does decide to do an interview. It's an attitude that makes him an attractive figure to his fans and, certainly, he appears to be irresistible to most women under the age of eighty. There is also a temper that is still spoken of with awe by those who witnessed it in its full, youthful flow when Fallon was an apprentice on the Curragh. But there's no evidence of that now as he gives a good quarter of an hour to questions about how it feels to be back, and how he thinks the appeal hearing will go. It's all remarkably cordial, in fact, until one of the jockeys going out for the next race has a little go. 'Take drugs and get your picture taken,' he sniffs.

If Fallon hears him, he doesn't let on. Admittedly, tucking into a colleague in front of a platoon of hacks wouldn't be the best public relations tactic, but there's also a palpable confidence there that the hearing will go his way.

'Where's the racing next week?' he grins at the English reporters, before admitting that he is very confident of the charges being dropped.

'Anything else, lads?' he eventually asks, and the huddle breaks up. Fallon steps back into the uncomplicated sanctuary of the jockeys-room and his pursuers rush to file stories.

Owing to an in camera ruling in London that forbids any of the British papers even referring to an appeal hearing, the cross-channel boys are reduced to reporting on a room containing a rather large elephant dancing around which they aren't allowed to mention. There are no such problems for the home brigade, much to the displeasure of the visitors.

'The judge said not to even refer to it.'

'Different jurisdiction, baby!'

There's so much colour, news and atmosphere to play with that time moves on rather too quickly. It's only while I'm in the middle of pondering why the always publicity-conscious Coolmore empire hasn't lost patience with it's wayward jockey that the reality of the third race being almost about to start hits home.

Fallon might be the story but Katirisa will be the Tipperary pay-off. On that sore evening at Naas when I was expensively playing bookmaker with Peeping Fawn, John Oxx's filly was the only one of the opposition that even briefly looked like saving the day. She came second to a classic runner. Tonight's mile maiden is the sort of logical step-up that a late-developing Aga Khan-bred filly should take in her stride. Unfortunately, everybody else seems to believe the same. In the ring, every trace of odds against has disappeared. There might be a little better on offer at Betfair, but not for €300. Evens will do at this stage, except everyone else has the same idea. Katirisa keeps edging back towards even money but never quite seems to make it.

It's decision time. Betting at even slightly odds-on just goes against the grain, but this is a *cojones* test. What are a couple of fractions? It's just a mental thing – illogical – and a bit of racecourse voodoo. Backing out of what, to all intents and purposes, must be a good-thing indicates a serious absence in the reproductive area. There's no choice which, of course, is a very bad reason to do anything.

Katirisa jumps well and Kinane has her just off the pace set by Many Colours, a filly that finished behind the favourite in that race at Naas. It all goes ideally to plan until the last couple of furlongs. Tipperary is an almost entirely flat track, the only one in the country. It rewards speed from the front which makes it hard for horses to come from behind. Katirisa is close enough to take the leader if she's good enough, but it quickly becomes obvious that she isn't. A hundred yards from the line, Kinane accepts it and Many Colours wins by two-and-a-half lengths.

That's €250 at 10–11 gone down the swanee. At least I made the bet, though, there was no pussy-footing around; I arrived at an opinion and backed it up: how terrible would it have been if she'd won unbacked? It was the right thing to do, which doesn't stop it feeling like a kick in those same *cojones*.

Running total: + €2,650

Triers to the Front

13 June 2007

There's no logical way that Many Colours should have beaten Katarisa. The fact that she did shows just how irrelevant the role of logic is in this game. Clearly, any expectation of deductive reasoning from half-a-tonne of animal with a brain the size of a small walnut is destined for disappointment but, even allowing for the fact that different distances produce different results, or that ground conditions can turn form on its head or that jockeys deliver crap rides, it's still rather disconcerting to realise that the large green formbook which outlines every detail of every race is often completely superfluous.

Take for instance that never-to-be-forgotten blub-fest when Mahler dragged some steaming chestnuts out of an open fire at Gowran. Strictly on form, that result was impossible. Vincenzio Galilei had eight lengths in hand from the race when both made their debuts. Mahler might have run in between times – and won – but a First in mathematics isn't necessary to deduce that Vincenzio was the form pick. However, not only was he beaten, he was beaten out of sight by fifteen lengths. That's a twenty-three length turn around. Ocean-going yacht races have been won by less. But the really significant part of it was that no one was surprised. Mahler was a heavily backed, odds-on shot, while Vincenzio drifted like a barge. Now, it should be pointed out that Mahler was as green as grass on his debut and has clearly improved hugely. But still form, like truth, is all in the perception.

It's not as if the game is bent any more: not really anyway. In fact, compared to fifteen or twenty years ago, the present day is a convent of purity and propriety. Back then, the form-book was like a heavily made-up hooker: things might have looked OK on the surface but underneath the plaster were cracks that couldn't have been filled in with a cement mixer. Reading it was an exercise in hooky psychology or, to put it more bluntly, guessing who was likely to be off on a certain day. Form still had some relevance to the major races but, for most of the rest of the stuff, it was about as useful as a jackhammer in a minefield.

The comedian and actor Niall Tobin tells the story about a well-to-do English owner bringing a horse to Ireland in order to pull the sort of touch that Tobin himself portrayed in the 1970s television drama *Murphy's Stroke*. After engaging one of the best stopping jockeys in the country, the Englishman enters a five-runner race and instructs the rider to finish third. This duly happens and, afterwards, the jockey is suitably impressed.

'A great horse, a great horse,' he informs the owner. 'It was all I could do to stop him winnin'. He was pullin' me arms out. Do you see them? They're stretched!'

'That's very good. And you're sure you could have beaten the two horses in front of you?'

'Ah, he'd have beaten the shite out of them. Did you not see me? Me arms were pulled out of their sockets.'

'Excellent.'

'The only thing is, I wouldn't be sure he'd beat the two behind me.'

That's an exaggeration, but not by much. Ireland in the early 1990s was a far cry from today and, with poor prize money, the only way to get a few bob out of owning a racehorse was by betting. Setting one up for 'the day' was what it was all about. Horses were stopped for months on end in order to secure or preserve a handicap mark for when they could be let off most profitably. Trainers built reputations on their ability to pull off strokes. Jockeys made livings out of stopping horses and some were so good they did nothing else. On one famous occasion, a starter having trouble getting the runners into line behind a tape, eventually threw his hands in the air and shouted, 'Triers to the front!' All this was carried out under the noses of some well-intentioned but non-combative stewards whose only qualification seemed to be that they had failed an eye test.

It didn't take long for any greenhorn to figure out that every race deserved a minimum of two looks. One to watch what was happening at the front and a replay to weed out the dodge-pots. The no-tries could sometimes be difficult to tell from the can't-tries but experience, and a bleary eye, soon narrowed the margins for error. An oldie, but a goldie, was the give-the-outside-to-nobody move, whereby a jockey took his horse to the outside of the field and gave away so much ground in the process that the beast would have to be a mixture of Shergar and Pegasus to compensate. Often, at some of the less well-policed country tracks, there was enough room on the rails for a tank regiment to get through – line abreast.

Sometimes, we were treated to the strangely gratifying sight of one who wasn't off a yard but still insisted on galloping fast enough to make a burying-it-out-of-sight-at-the-back job impossible. Faced with such a problem, the jockey was usually forced to find a series of obstacles in his path. Any pocket was filled quicker than polyfilla; any mass rank of equine backsides to run up against was gratefully availed of. And if that didn't work, there was always the option of just taking a good old-fashioned tug and hope the stewards were holding their binoculars back to front. Some guys went by the post with their mouths only slightly less open than the horses that were carting them towards a date with a suspension.

In practically any other country, the crowd would have been waiting for these merchants with ropes, but here, apart from a few shouts, there was usually nothing but indulgence. Which was understandable really: it's not as if the jocks were doing it just for kicks, they were simply doing what they were told.

Of course, it's a different story now that the country is

awash with money, but to believe that increased wealth means a consequent decline in stroke-play is clearly ridiculous. It's unusual for a meeting to go by without at least one case of a run that is usually, and euphemistically, described as 'eye-catching'. The more flamboyant examples usually provoke the high-dudgeon brigade into letter-writing form, usually wielding the last-known pens filled with green ink. Their more computer-literate brethren don't waste time with snail-mail and immediately vent their spleen on chat rooms. Words like 'blatant', 'disgrace' and 'shameful' bounce around the information super-highway – and right and proper that is too. The miracle, when you think about it, is that they haven't got more to write about.

There are races being run at midweek gaff meetings that regularly see betting turnover of over €500,000 on Betfair. That's ridiculously out of proportion to what is actually going on out on the track. Most of the time, €500,000 would buy every single runner at the races with enough left over to purchase the racecourse itself. It's even worse during the winter when the weather can cut into the programme and punters end up being grateful for the chance to bet their brains out on Wolverhampton or Downpatrick. With nothing else available, seven-figure amounts will be matched on horses that aren't even worth five figures. And with that sort of money floating around, it's inevitable that people are going to do the maths and compare what's on offer in prize money with what can be got with just a little bit of imagination.

In such circumstances, conspiracy theories abound. There are punters who will argue that every single stage of most races is choreographed before the start. This rather ignores the reality that eight-and-a-half stone of human being can hardly be relied upon to place half-a-tonne of highly toned animal exactly where he wants every time, but to point this out usually leads to being dismissed as naïve. The reality is that enough happens on a racecourse to make any kind of crazy theory sound at least mildly plausible for a while. Another reality is that most theories are just ways of avoiding the fact that we've messed up – it's always easier to blame someone else.

Right now, though, at almost nine o'clock on a Wednesday evening at Leopardstown, there's no getting away from one certainty – I have to back a horse this week. Westlake is the ideal. He's running in a three-year-old maiden over a mile-and-a-half and, although twelve line up, only one of the others is a realistic threat. The ground is perfect, so is the trip and the stable is in form. On his last start, the bay colt with the big white blaze was third to Mahler which is far better form than anything else can boast. In contrast, the threat, Honolulu, has run just once and that was when starting 8–1 for a maiden at Roscommon where he finished only third. If he was trained by anyone else except Aidan O'Brien, he would be a double-figure price. As it is, there's enough money floating around for him to keep Westlake at nearly 6–4 odds. It's set up for Dermot Weld's horse, and for a slightly desperate wannabe punter in big need of a big score.

Reassuringly, there are some familiar faces down here in the ring at the same time, all with the same predatory gaze directed at the bookmakers' boards, and all walking down the line with that intent stride that dissuades anyone from even thinking of stopping for a chat. Virgil is among them, in more casual gear tonight but with that mobile phone clamped to his ear. Some of the other serious guys are here too, which is encouraging. This really is a punters race. Only two can win: it's just a case of picking right.

It's a gloomy evening and the bright red figures on the boards take on an extra sheen, drawing us all even closer. They work too, suddenly Westlake's price starts falling rapidly. Any 6–4 is a distant memory and, quickly, so too is 5–4. Within seconds, a lot of those bright lights have turned to evens. Honolulu might be fancied but it's Westlake that the serious guys want. That's the cue: the last of the 11–10 is about to disappear but with a surge that an All Black second-row forward would be proud of, only a small number of people are trampled in order to secure €330 to €300. The other €300 I hang on to.

Normally, such caution is not advisable and it's certainly the wrong step now. The serious guys will see a price they're satisfied with and take it, but a fear of ending up with less than the very best odds available means I wind up hoping for a late rush on Honolulu, which will push Westlake out again. It doesn't happen. Instead the Weld horse tightens into odds-on.

The extra half of my biggest bet of the year starts to feel a little soggy. It may be voodoo but, after Katirisa, the idea of more odds-on is enough to provoke sweaty palms. The horses are starting to load when a colleague appears. He's got some interesting news, having spoken to Dermot Weld.

'I was talking to DK earlier. I asked him straight about this horse.'

'Yeah?'

'He says he should win. But he had a cough a while ago

and that's why he hasn't run for a while. He might come on for it. I got the impression he's not too confident.'

So now, there are two flip-of-the-coin decisions to make. One is Westlake versus Honolulu. The other is 'says he should win' versus 'not too confident'. It's a genuine agony of indecision but, thankfully, not one that lasts long. With the last couple loading, David Power offers evens about Westlake. 'Should win' triumphs easily.

Then comes the prolonged agony of watching Westlake lose.

The worst part is that there's no one else to blame. There isn't even too much actual blame to apportion. A choice of two and my pick is wrong. Almost everyone else picked wrong too, or else the horse wouldn't be favourite. Not everyone else has had their biggest bet of the year, though, not everyone else presumed that collecting would be as easy as going down and coming back.

There's a horrible feeling of inevitability about it from the start. Kieren Fallon, still reeling from the recent failure of his appeal bid, is not normally one to make the running but he's determined this time. It reeks of a plan to search out any vulnerability in the favourite. Westlake, travelling in mid-division, is slightly hampered coming out of the back straight and then smoothly makes ground on the turn in. If you were to be hypercritical, you could argue that he has to make up a little too much ground too quickly, but that's just splitting hairs. Pat Smullen delivers him to win, Westlake eyeballs his rival but simply can't get past. He gets sustained pressure from the saddle for the first time in his life and, fifty yards from the line, it all becomes too much. The horse wobbles to his right and, with the rail to help him, Honolulu is half a length too good.

Walking back to the parade ring, the post-race band cranks into ear-splitting gear and displays a nice line in irony.

'Cel-e-brate good times – COME ON!'

The blonde singer would normally be enough to rouse the instincts of a blind castrato, but not now. It would be nice to say that losing €600 like this is met with a quiet, dignified stoicism: just a slight quiver of the lip while I light a cheroot and button up against the sudden night chill. Yes, that would be nice. But, instead, it's no exaggeration to say it's a struggle to put one foot in front of the other. Something will have to be done about this; these emotional swingboats are too much. Going from Bee Gee strut to Leonard Cohen with a limp is wearing beyond belief. There's no future in it either: the top jockeys always say it's important not to get too high when winning or too low when losing. What Dettori must be like to live with on the bad days must be unbelievable.

'It's up to you – what's your pleasurahh – everyone around the world – COME ON!'

Right now, I feel like texting home and warning everyone to keep their heads down, which is selfish. But, most of all, I feel like I'm running like a demented rabbit just to stand still. This is getting nowhere.

Running total: + €1,850

The Tall, Thin Buddha

25 June

It's a grubby exercise – surfing the net to find the promise of instant gratification – but desperation can make anyone do funny things. There's no other way to explain why the following words are suddenly ready to enter into the Google search engine, mocking with their yearning – 'books on betting'.

There are plenty of them and all guarantee different varieties of a promised land. On amazon.co.uk, the various summaries have the sort of pitches that conjure feverish dreams of magical systems paying off – or make that 'could' pay off, or 'may' pay off, or have the 'potential' to pay off. They might even be right. But there's only one thing that's certain – nobody who ever came up with a system that really paid off has ever had the financial imperative to commit it to print.

There are 'how to' books on everything. When you open a Betfair account, they even send you a *Winning on Betfair for Dummies* book – it's part of the well-known series. If you get tired of endlessly making money on the exchanges, there's also the option of *Jewellery Making and Beading for Dummies*, *Knitting for Dummies* and the one that's definitely next on my list, *Statistics for Dummies*. I want to find out if it's statistically possible that a snowball has more chance of surviving the summer underneath John McCririck's buttocks than this dummy has of backing a winner on Betfair.

None of this, of course, has anything do with Betfair itself. Indeed, for those of us who watch most of our racing on the TV, it's a wondrous facility. But just as every punter realises there are certain bookies who will get everything beaten, there is mounting and compelling evidence that pressing that blue Bet button is a jinx to make the Hope Diamond seem like a household trinket.

There is no rational reason for this, but, since we have already dismissed the role of reason, let's indulge instinct for a while. It's not a technological problem – although it does say something that for a country so pleased with itself for being on the frontline of computer development a person can live just twenty-five miles from the centre of the capital city and still have a broadband signal so weak that logging on takes up to five minutes. One learns to live with such minor irritations. After all, the headquarters of RTÉ, the national broadcaster, is even closer and manages to transmit a signal that provides a very pleasant display of snow throughout the year.

There's certainly nothing wrong with the value on offer either. Horses that are outside, say, the first four in the betting are often double the price on offer from bookmakers. There are options available that make betting in shops or in the ring look positively stone age in comparison. And yet, at the races, my first instinct when serious about a horse is to head to the ring. Maybe that's simply years of habit, but there may also be more to it.

Make no mistake – there are ways to win on the exchange that are almost foolproof. The real disciplinarians bet the margins, dealing in thousands in order to come up with a fifty or a hundred quid profit on each play. The method is simple enough: these guys spend the day glued to their computer screen, trying to figure out which way a horse, usually the favourite, is going to go in the betting. If they believe the indications are that it will shorten in price, they will back it. A drifter will be a lay. Then, they bet the opposite way. If a horse is backed first, then the sharp guys will try and lay the same horse for slightly more than they backed it. The result is that they can't lose. The margin might be no more than €20 or €30, but do that ten times a day and you're well ahead.

Except, how awful an existence is that? How socially inadequate must someone be to do that day-in, day-out and not go stark, staring bonkers, just sitting on the couch, fiddling with their mouse. Statistically, it would be an interesting experiment to find out how many of these people are called Leonard, wear glasses and own girlfriends that have to be folded up and packed away. There might be a significant profit in trading up that margin. It would fit in too because, for the Leonards of this world, it doesn't actually matter what happens in the races. They're just a vehicle for predicting where the edge is. Whether you trade in oil, money, figs or Hong Kong lady-boys, the mechanics are just the same. However, city types at least get the chance to wear sharp suits. Depending on the size of their portfolios, they are also allowed to wrap their tongues around women with names like Fenella and Marisa. The only things our shrewdies get their tongues around usually come in boxes and are delivered by Chinese men on small motorcycles.

A lot of racecourse punters who fancy they are ahead of the game possess many of the same social-skill levels as their homebound brethren, but at least they have the opportunity for some contact with functioning humanity. That can be vital in maintaining a toehold on planet earth while still expending a substantial part of your life in the pursuit of so-called easy money. It's those of us marooned at home who are in far greater danger of suddenly finding ourselves regularly ringing the buxom woman with the see-through panties in the chatroom advert – just to talk.

Routine is an enemy at the best of times but, with something like this, it's a dangerous enemy. Three months into this project, there is an undeniable sameness creeping in, and not just in terms of losing – it's starting to take over the entire day.

The first task of each morning is to get the *Racing Post*, which is an essential. Considering it doesn't have any competition, the game's bible is a superb production, providing more information than is probably strictly good for any one person. Still, it can't be faulted for allowing people choice. A quick glance at the Irish racing form guides is followed by a closer examination of the analysis of each race from the day before. Some of these are only partially available because the paper has to be put to bed halfway through the evening meetings. But since the flat races are usually run first at the many mixed cards run in Ireland, that isn't a problem. These bits are especially useful for finding out if a beaten horse came back lame or sick. After that, it's a simple case of reading all the news. That might appear nothing, but it's remarkable how little nuggets of information can percolate in and become useful weeks later. Something simple – like a trainer dismissing a future race as too difficult for a still-immature prospect – can become important.

Then, at 9.30 a.m. religiously, the attheraces channel is switched on for their racing review. This shows all the previous day's racing again in what is an easy and convenient space filler for them and an important chance for anyone who might have been unable to prise the remote control away from a SpongeBob lover the previous evening to actually watch the races.

It's hard to overstate the impact that daily televised racing has had. In the past, serious betting by anyone unable to go to every race meeting must have been impossible. Actually being able to watch how your horse runs is pretty funda-mental but, even twenty years ago, the betting-shop industry managed to thrive on a commentary service that sounded as if it was coming from a depth-charged U-boat heading for the bottom. A 20 per cent betting tax was also in place and yet any shop you ever went into was almost always full. It was a triumph of hope over adversity, and possibly a good way to stay out of the rain.

Now there's zero tax and, for less than thirty quid a month, the basic Sky satellite package brings racing from every corner of the globe. It's truly a wondrous and brave new world. The only problem is that it's still a bastard trying to win.

A perk of the journalistic gig is the facility to work from home so, by 10.30 a.m., when the following day's runners are available, full wakefulness isn't that far away. Three months into this project, however, and that initial falling-on-the-form-like-a-hungry-hyena enthusiasm has been replaced by something altogether more dutiful. To suggest it is becoming a grinding chore would be to insult an awful lot of people working in the real world, so let's just say the repetition of it all has become somewhat soporific. It's noticeable, however, that it now only takes a glance to size-up the general shape of most races. All this diligent attention means the names are becoming more and more familiar. Before, at some of the more nondescript meetings, there were races that contained lists of horses that may as well have spent their careers on the moon. Now, if the thing has shown any level of form, there's a fair chance that I can distinguish it from other members of the animal kingdom without puzzled recourse to the formbook.

Nevertheless, it is possible to get through an entire day lost in form and a fog of technology: switching from the computer to the television, back to the internet and on to the phone while, all the time, keeping an eye on what's happening on the exchanges. After a while, it becomes mind-numbing. The TV becomes a drone in the corner. Press the mute button and there's a hum from the computer that hints at some action bubbling online that just has to be checked out. It's a completely artificial existence, a virtual world of glowing digits and endless opportunity to do your dough – and there is a soullessness to it that can't be good.

This is not supposed to be a dry, academic exercise in number crunching. After all, behind every set of form figures and each handicap mark is a living, breathing creature in a box, munching its head off and crapping in the corner. Presuming to predict exactly what it will do among a herd of others is a conceit on our part that deserves every financial hit we get. In fact, parse it right down and it's ludicrous putting substantial sums of money on the outcome of a race that could well depend more on the state of an animal's digestive system than on any convoluted theories of ground, weight, distance and breeding. It's time to step back into reality.

***

Even at the best of times, the Curragh on a Monday morning in late June is never going to be mistaken for Marbella. But it's still a shock to see it looking so grim. Rain is teeming down so hard that the roads around the huge plain are starting to flood. It could be February, except for the daylight. A cold wind makes thousands of shorn sheep look nostalgic for their wool as they press against the enormous clumps of green gorse which are the only things interrupting the flatness. This is the reality of working with horses: chilblains even during the summer.

Massive white marquees are parked in front of the racecourse ready for the Derby in six days' time. At 7 a.m., those working on the new ringroad and the buildings being constructed at the back of the Curragh are already scurrying like yellow, hard-hatted ants. There was a time when working with horses meant being the first up. In this new and better Ireland, no one can afford to sleep in.

Compared to the neat orderliness of its equivalent at Newmarket, the Curragh always feels a lot more elemental. The first horses emerging for exercise on the Kildare town side make their way towards an all-weather gallop that snakes through thick gorse. The sheep glance disinterestedly at the expensively bred creatures cantering past without a restrictive running rail or barrier to stop them galloping for miles into the distance if they choose to go Tonto.

A couple of miles away, it's a different story as a large string of horses make for the Old Vic gallop, their riders hunched against the elements. It's striking as they trot past how diverse the range of voices and faces are.

Economic prosperity means that more Irish people now enjoy their racing from the corporate box rather than the 'factory floor' of the racing yard. When the guys mixing cement just a few hundred yards away are making more money for less danger, there's always the temptation to look at the ornery creature just waiting to cart you off into the distance and decide there are easier ways to make a living. There can't be a yard in Ireland now that doesn't have its share of work riders from South America, Eastern Europe and many other places around the world. The evidence is there as a lollipop man stops traffic heading towards the M8 in order to let the string cross the road towards the gallops. Skin more used to the glow of São Paulo or Cordoba mixes with the more usual pinched paleness as the string silently passes impatient commuters. The lollipop man, however, gets a quiet word from one rider, '*Obrigado.*'

There is more colourful language from an older man towards the rear as the horse underneath him starts jig-jogging and tossing its head in the air. The animal is told off in a broad Kildare accent but the rider's hands never change on the reins. In that mysterious language called horseman-ship, he manages to get the colt back into line and moving forward without hardly breaking step. Such skill can make all the difference in the mental development of a delicate athlete and this guy has a face which has experience etched all over it. It must be a tough gig, however, for a man kicking on in years to have to face the elements every morning while cajoling half-a-tonne of animal from a saddle no bigger than a napkin. There are surely easier ways to make a living, but, as the horses pair off and start up the gallop, I feel a pang of jealousy that confirms there are probably few ways that are more exciting.

Even from hundreds of yards away, the surge of power as the horses start galloping is intoxicating. There's a barely controlled elasticity to these animals that must make riding them feel like being perched on top of a twister.

Unfortunately for those of us rooted to terra firma through a combination of too little skill and too much funk, it will forever be a mystery. No doubt, that old man thundering past would do himself a mischief laughing at the idea that there might be something touching on the mystical about staying on the back of a dumb animal. But most of us only value what we can't do – and maybe he was consumed with envy at my ability to dive out of the way of Dermot Weld's jeep.

DK has his game face on. His long, spare figure is curled around the steering wheel as he careers through puddles. His objective is the end of the long, all-weather gallop where he can stand and watch and listen as the horses go by. There's a resolute determination in his eyes that doesn't augur well for any rider who fails to go the speed or the distance they've been told to.

Everyone has a version of themselves that they like to present to the world, the one they like to be judged on, and the great trainer is no different. DK's speciality is a rather patrician indulgence punctuated by generous bursts of smiling charm. As he gets older, there is also an increasingly sage-like quality to the man. Like some tall, thin Buddha perched at the centre of all he surveys around the Curragh, Weld appears never to be surprised. When his horses win, they are greeted with a gentle pat on the neck and a nod that indicates everything is as it should be with the world.

There are other faces, apparently, as befits someone with flint-like intelligence and a business ability that is the stuff of legend. Those who deal with him regularly in the buying and selling of horses will tell you that Weld can make John Magnier look as innocent as a schoolgirl. The last one to sell him a pup was probably showing them in a box, and it's unlikely that there was much profit in it. At the same time, however, there is a sentimentality there that doesn't quite fit with the ruthless businessman. He takes an almost childish delight in setting records – and in letting you know about them. He has also repeatedly expressed a desire to give up training and start writing books, which everybody but nobody expects to happen any time soon. It all adds up to a complicated sum of a man who is unquestionably the most intriguing personality in the game.

As with most genuinely fascinating characters, nobody in racing seems to have a bland, middle-of-the-road opinion of him. There are a few who appear ready to cut his throat; others are just plain awestruck and some simply resent him for his success. Part of that resentment is a result of Weld's media profile.

'You guys like him because he talks to you,' is the rather sniffy attitude of another Curragh trainer who seems quick to dismiss his neighbour as a shameless self-promoter.

It's an odd criticism, not so much because Weld doesn't try to play the press as much on his own terms as he can, but rather because he should somehow wait for someone else to do the job for him. Around here, in this open-air cauldron of gossip and rumour, he would be waiting a long time. It's also strange to expect us media types to ignore him since we're talking about someone who is possessed of more than a touch of genius so, while Weld may pick and choose the sides of himself he wishes the world to see, he can hardly blame us for trying to find out how he ticks.

This is a man who has genuinely changed the face of a sport throughout the world. He remains the only non-America-based trainer to win an American classic. Vintage Crop's 1993 victory in the Melbourne Cup was a success of such original skill that it ranks among the very greatest sporting achievements ever produced by Ireland. In fact, Weld has the sort of vision that politicians would kill for. But watching him now, disappearing into the dark skyline at a rate of knots, the only wonder is where he gets the time.

There must be forty horses belting up the gallop and this is just the first lot of the day. There will probably be a couple more before the morning's through. In terms of logistics alone, organising this moving sea of humanity and animals would be a challenge to Eisenhower. To then calculate what each animal needs to produce its best – over what distance and ground, and what time of the season – before then figuring out how to bring it to peak fitness is a challenge that would reduce most of us to gibbering wrecks. Throw in soothing the personalities of millionaire owners, who believe success is commensurate with the size of their egos, and you have a recipe for a busy working life. That Weld can do this and still come across all suavely casual when he wants is an achievement in itself.

The long line gallops through the gloom, displaying all the keyed-up health of athletes at the peak of their game. Among them are a couple of greys. The Weld runner in the Derby in six days' time is Prince Erik, who is almost white in colour. One of them might be him. Or it might not. That's the problem with us enthusiasts – unless we know already, we don't know. The top professionals can look at a regiment of horses and see everything important in seconds. Weld is famously able to distinguish each and every one of his string, and he can do it from at least a mile away through a mist. That's the thing that even the most jealous of his colleagues cannot dispute. If there's any semblance of talent there, he will get it out.

But even he can get it spectacularly wrong sometimes. It's some years ago now but, at one of the Tralee August festivals, Weld volunteered a tip to the press pack.

'Iron County Xmas will win,' he said, delivering one of those little nods that suggest it has now been decreed and so it shall be done.

Not surprisingly, some luxuriantly proportioned arses were just a blur in the direction of the betting ring. Iron County Xmas started a well-backed second-favourite and finished pulled up – in a flat race! Maybe it's churlish to dig it up now, but it would also be dishonest not to record our bemusement at the great man managing to get it so spectacularly wrong. It still feels unsettling because, if Weld can do that, what the hell chance is there for anyone else?

Standing out here in a mini-hurricane is certainly not achieving much in any concrete sense. DK is hardly going to spot the lone hack in the distance, mosey on over for a chat and spoon-feed three or four winners for the weekend. All around is the evidence of people getting on with their lives. The horses file past after their work and it's impossible to hear them over the roar of all the traffic passing by and the constant drone from the massive building site nearby. In comparison, I must look about as useful as a spare member in the royal enclosure.

However, there's no doubt the morning has been of benefit. Maybe it's a result of a temporary release from the technological tyranny at home, but there could hardly be a greater contrast than this earthy back-to-basics and the mathematical puzzles of the formbook. Watching these wonderfully beautiful, but infuriatingly vulnerable, animals up close is a timely reminder of how unscientific the whole exercise of getting a horse to the races really is. Every one of them is only a funny step away from losing – or worse. That realisation should make the practice of trying to find winners even more daunting, but actually it helps.

Anyone putting down even a 50¢ yankee expects to win. There's no other reason to have the bet in the first place. But once it is down, no amount of mathematical theory or macho posturing can disguise how each punter is throwing his money and hopes into the sky with little or no control over where fate decides they'll land. Planning and strategy are for the deluded. An educated guess is the best anyone can make, no matter how much they want to believe otherwise.

It's a relief to be reminded.

Running total: + €1,200

Power Sharing Doesn't Work

1 July

Lisvale is a two-year-old colt that, right now, looks magnificent. As he pads around the Curragh parade ring on the first evening of the Derby festival, it's impossible not to stare at him. No doubt, professionals who know what they're inspecting will crib at some part of his conformation but, from a less-expert point of view, Lisvale is the clear pick of the seventeen runners. It's a health thing. This still-immature little horse is radiating the stuff. From the sheen on his coat to the alert cock of his ears, Lisvale looks more than a little pleased with himself. He also looks more than a little ready to win.

It's a hot race, however, this opening seven-furlong maiden. The favourite, Pittori, was only just beaten by a

Royal Ascot winner on his only start. Aidan O'Brien has two newcomers, one of them, a flashy looking Montjeu colt called Alessandro Volta, is, supposedly, the second string since Fallon isn't on board but is also regarded as being potentially very smart indeed. He's got the look of his sire all right, a tall, imposing customer with a mix of arrogance and volatility in his expensively bred eye.

Despite that hauteur, Lisvale's still the one. A lot of people spend a lot of money on a lot of chemicals in an attempt to feel as good as he clearly does right now. Unlike his grandiosely monickered rival, he also has the advantage of having run before and there was enough in it to have had more than a few of us watching him finally grasp the requirements of the job in the final stages and jot his name down in that famously metaphorical 'notebook'.

There is also the considerable plus that Lisvale is trained by David Wachman – a trainer so hot this season that he is in danger of leaving scorch marks. Since he supplied Potion to win that day at Naas, the man is already guaranteed a place in my affections but she is just one of a steady stream of winners for the obviously bright thirty-six-year-old. Even without his timely financial assistance, it's easy to feel happy for Wachman. He has an attractive mix of personality and resolution that promises to make him a figure of substance for a long time to come. He is even being mentioned as the next in line at Ballydoyle. Of course, personal warmth is hardly a prerequisite for success: Pittori's trainer Jim Bolger, for instance, has become a true giant of the game and has done it on charm of a more haemorrhoidal strain.

However, even turning into Cary Grant incarnate will not

persuade some people to rate Wachman. Virgil, for instance, won't back any of his horses, an indulgence that must be proving quite expensive. It's unfair, but hardly surprising, that the prejudice exists. The fact that Wachman is married to John Magnier's daughter is enough to have the envious and the cynical leaping to conclusions, but before his father-in-law started putting horses in training with him, the young man from Kildare had already carved out a healthy training profile all on his lonesome.

A bet of €700 to €100 is an expression of faith in Wachman getting it right again.

As the race begins, Pittori is favourite and Alessandro Volta is being wildly backed while his stable companion drifts like Woody Guthrie in a barge. Normally securing some cover up the long straight is preferable at the Curragh but Lisvale and Pittori appear ready to dismiss such subtleties. They are at the head of the field – there to be shot at – and staring the big, bald Curragh square in the eye. Neither of them even comes close to flinching. The rest of the field might have a couple of targets to shoot at but from well over a furlong out, it is obvious none of them will get to the two in front. It really is an eyeball to eyeball. For juveniles, it's a serious test. Both jockeys spare nothing. They flash past the post in a blur of speed that can't stop the colon-scouring suspicion that Lisvale has just been touched off. Why wasn't the bet each way? If it was, there would have been €175 coming back – on top of the €700!

If someone had offered any sort of price on Pittori in the few seconds before the result was announced, the whole shooting match would have gone on. His nose was in front just before and just after the line but, Good Lord a'mighty, it ain't there when it counts. There was a time when calling photos was easy but time seems to have moved on with a consequent impact on eyesight – thankfully.

Just minutes later, Virgil, the man who stressed the importance of looking at the contenders in the parade ring, literally bumps past. Even by his usual standards, he seems in a rush. There's an angle to his walk that suggests 'here's my jaw and my arse will be here in a minute'.

'Oh,' he says. 'How're you doing?'

'Not too bad: had that last winner in fact.'

'Me too.'

'I thought you didn't back Wachman horses.'

'The way they're running, he's got a reprieve!'

Virgil looks in the sort of hurry that suggests he has forgotten to turn off the immersion but he still hangs around for a minute going through the card. It's a curious exercise, him volunteering a little and waiting for a more effusive response. After a while, it dawns that he's actually pumping for information. It's a compliment, of sorts. Whatever he gets is greeted with the sort of indifference that suggests he's already heard it – but still he persists. It's not that he wants to hear what I think but what I might have heard that matters.

'This O'Brien filly in the Listed might shake up the favourite,' he says, *sotto voce*. 'I don't know if she has the speed though. She's bred to be a stayer.'

'Apparently, she's showing a lot of speed at home,' I answer, eagerly trying to give the impression this isn't ninth-hand information fortuitously overheard in the weigh room.

'Hmm,' is the only response, but it's enough to provoke an

interesting little tidbit. 'The last race is a bad maiden but, apparently, Weld thinks his best chance this evening is this Power Sharing. It ran a funny race at Naas.'

That 'funny race' was seven weeks ago when Power Sharing went off like a bat out of hell from the stalls before eventually finishing well behind. The bare form is nothing but Virgil is right about it being a bad race tonight. The favourite, Red Rock Canyon, is one of those impeccably bred horses that shows enough talent to tantalise but appears to lack sufficient spine to follow through on it. Apart from him, and maybe one or two others, the rest look nothing. A few queries back in the weigh room result in a couple of behind-the-racecard conversations which confirm that Power Sharing is, indeed, fancied but might not be a customer to trust with too much money.

Apparently, he is unstable enough to have made Fred West seem pretty damn healthy: he likes biting other horses and any creature, man or beast, crazy enough to get within spitting distance is instantly lined up as target practice for a wicked pair of back legs.

'A headcase,' declares one helpful informant.

'Are you going to back him?'

'Fucking sure I am. Look at what's happened to him since the last day.'

A glance at the racecard reveals a single letter that is provoking quite a lot of greedy anticipation. The 'g' under Power Sharing's name stands for gelding, a state not usually appreciated by the male gender of any species, since it results in the absence of a pair of rather prized items from the large family pack. However, the removal of one's best friends has a long and honourable tradition of diverting even the horniest equine mind away from the joy of sex and make it concentrate on running faster for longer. Maybe it has now done the same for this loon. It also doesn't hurt that he's grey – by now, any belief in coincidence should have disappeared, but, still, the idea that Power Sharing may have been one of the greys I saw on the gallops earlier in the week brings in a groovy karma kind of vibe.

The mood isn't dampened when Listen reproduces the speed she has been showing at home and makes a winning debut in the Listed race. €50 at 4–1 makes it a €900 profit night so far. Now is surely the time to invest in the absence of Power Sharing's testicles.

There's a sniff of 14–1 that lasts no time at all and a couple of hundred at 12–1 is the best available. Missing out on the best price always leaves a bad taste but, in this case, it doesn't last for long because the 12–1 doesn't last any time either. Leaving the ring, there's a struggle to get any more than tens. A quick check on Betfair reveals a different story. A luminous blue twenty stares out. It's just for €20 but that will deliver the same as Listen. Another €10 goes on at 16.5. That must be a reflection of what's happening outside: except it isn't. A couple of minutes later and it's possible to get on €20 more at 24.0 and another €20 at 19.3. By the time the horses reach the start, Power Sharing is available at 13–1, a full five points better than his starting price. There's a close-on €4,000 pay-off if he wins.

The problem is that the wrong piece of anatomy has been removed from Power Sharing. It should have been his brain. At the start, he looks like he's about to spontaneously combust. It's not because of nerves or anxiety: what he clearly wants is a fight. Stroppily skipping round in circles, he quickly clears a big area of ground into which none of the other horses and jockeys are silly enough to venture. Pat Smullen has his feet out of the irons and resembles a pale leaf being carted around on a bolshy breeze.

Power Sharing breaks well and for five of the ten furlongs actually manages to give a reasonable impression of a race-horse. The others around him don't look particularly thrilled at the proximity of this grey head-banger but, luckily for them, they don't have to put up with it for long. The idea of running downhill and putting in a bit of effort is clearly repulsive. At halfway, Smullen proves there's nothing wrong with his bottle and decides to deliver a few serious belts with his whip. Not many would be surprised if the horse reacted to this by turning round and spitting in the jockey's eye, which would be fine if he kept running but, instead, the only thing he spits is the dummy. He tails in well beaten and, no doubt, pleased that he's proved to be his own man – even without the equipment.

The entire weekend is like this.

On Saturday, there's no action really, except to watch Peeping Fawn win the Group 1 Pretty Polly Stakes. She's heavily backed to beat a field that includes the French Oaks winner and she does it in no little style. There's no point backing her in anything now. It would just be a hex on a filly who is rapidly turning into the very best of her generation. Neither of us needs the pain.

Derby day itself is different. Finding the winner is hard but the one certainty is that it won't be the favourite, Eagle

Mountain. He might have finished runner up at Epsom but stamina looks to be an issue with him, especially on ground that has more in common with Cheltenham in winter than a midsummer classic. Eagle Mountain is a clear favourite and an easy pick for Fallon from the four Ballydoyle runners. But this horse has never been totally convincing. Every instinct screams he can't win. Unfortunately, every instinct also screams not to go near those pink bars on Betfair.

My confidence is shot on the exchange. Trying to find a winner is impossible. No way does my morale need another Peeping Fawn job and, besides, there's a more likely betting option before the big race.

Because of the ground conditions, only four runners line up for the Railway Stakes. Two of them are from Ballydoyle and Fallon looks to have chosen absolutely right with South Dakota. The horse had no chance at Royal Ascot owing to a bad draw and he has form on ground with a little dig in it. To say that today's surface has a little dig is an understatement, but that bit of experience is more than the other three have. South Dakota isn't even favourite – Irish Jig has that privilege – but this simply looks like a massive blunder by the bookies. It's time to take advantage with some €700 to €400.

There are occasions when I would desperately love to shed around eight stone in order to ride the horse myself and not to have to make excuses for losing, and then there are other times when adding another eight to get some extra bone-breaking power seems desirable. It takes just over a minute to run six furlongs at the Curragh and that's ample opportunity to experience both emotions.

Criticising jockeys for losing will always be dismissed as

talking through a pocket. Slag off too much and the easy pop back is to ask how many winners you've had. Both arguments have some surface validity, but take this to its logical conclusion, and you could have some cocky little apprentice telling Peter O'Sullevan that he knows nothing about racing. But sometimes a ride is so cack-handed that it can send you running for somewhere high to jump from, and Fallon's effort on South Dakota is one of those occasions.

In a four-horse race, with a substantial part of Kildare on either side of him, he still manages to find interference that costs him the race. His stable companion, Lizard Island, is setting a funereal pace in front with South Dakota sitting last. That's hardly the smartest tactic off a slow pace anyway, but then Fallon decides to make his move between the two other runners. There's an inevitability to what happens next that has me shouting, 'No, no, no!' Both John Murtagh and Wayne Lordan close the gap and Fallon has to momentarily snatch up. Over six furlongs, such things spell the end. Switched to the outside, South Dakota finishes well but is less than a length shy of Lizard Island at the line. It's enough to make you weep.

Fallon chooses wrong in the Derby as well, but does nothing wrong. Eagle Mountain is third just behind Alexander Of Hales in second. Soldier Of Fortune, however, is nine lengths ahead of the pair of them and passes the post in splendid isolation to complete a clean sweep for Aidan O'Brien. It's some achievement, and the fourth time he's done it in an Irish classic. It also shows how a slavish devotion to form is a one-way ticket to skintville. Soldier Of Fortune was fifth at Epsom, well behind Eagle Mountain. Today, there's a good fifteen-length turnaround and, according to O'Brien, the reason is that Soldier Of Fortune has learned how to look at the bright side of life.

'He was very narky in himself before Epsom but, since then, he's been doing his work with a smile on his face,' explains the master horseman.

Even rucked around him in the sort of tight maul that would have Martin Johnson's eyes watering, there is a collective swivelling of the hack pack's eyes: Aidan sometimes comes out with such statements. On one memorable occasion at Gowran Park, a horse called Tchaikovsky was winning a race easily only to swerve dramatically in the final few yards.

'He was only shying away from the tiger,' O'Brien declared afterwards.

Those of us present who had watched the race on television in the weigh room were left wondering if the pressure had finally got to O'Brien. There were even some mildly condescending enquiries about where he might be taking some holidays – soon. But the explanation was simple, and a bust for the lazy sods who hadn't gone out to watch from the stands. The race was sponsored by Esso and some 'morketing' genius had decided to put a giant, inflatable tiger the size of Montmartre just behind the finishing post. Not unreasonably, Tchaikovksy took one look at the thing and voted to take a swerve.

That tiger comment, however, was typical of the straight-forward directness that O'Brien employs when discussing horses. There isn't a trace of irony in the way he patiently explains his belief that Soldier Of Fortune's face, and his ability, has been transformed by going to work smiling.

'Anyone who works with horses knows they have expressions just like people,' he says.

He's possibly being a little generous. There are more than a few chancers out there glorying in the job description of trainer who lack even the most basic self-awareness, never mind a knowledge about the subtleties of equine psychoanalysis.

What Derby day does indicate, though, is that even the chancers are getting wrapped up in the general feel-good factor that is keeping racing in Ireland toasty and warm right now. This is the day when the game collectively gives itself a pat on the back. The Derby brings together the great and the good from home and overseas and enables them to congratulate Irish racing and all who sail in her. There might be a damp edge to the weather but the condensation that's rising from the Curragh carries an unmistakably smug scent. Never before has the sport and the industry known better times. This really is a golden era and a home clean sweep in the big race is just the latest proof of that.

You'd have to be a prince among prigs to look at the crowd's determination to enjoy the day and not raise a smile. The Irish Derby is the one attempt that racing here has at creating a social scene that might, on any level, compare to Royal Ascot in England. There's a conscious effort being made to target whatever 'it' crowd happens to be 'it' right now, although it is a fact that nothing dates faster than trendiness. The result is a curious blend of die-hard racing fans, once-a-year merchants who wouldn't know a racehorse from an orang-utan and, of course, a social elite which is in possession of the most vital and glamorous element of all – money.

And there is a lot of wealth mooching around. A number of sheikhs sombrely march from the parade ring with bodyguards sporting bulges under their jackets. Many more home-grown squireens have the sort of women in tow that cost an awful lot of money to run, and confident trans-Atlantic accents loudly proclaim the place to be 'charming', although there should be some sort of reward for living in a climate like this. It's all rather pleasingly cosmopolitan. Everyone, though, regardless of their bank balance, has an eye out for the nearest shelter should the next shower sneak up without warning. Even the Aga Khan quickens his pace when it starts teeming down, no doubt looking forward to when the new €100 million stands are in place.

The Aga kick-started the Curragh reconstruction some years ago when he forked out about €15 million to buy the hotel at the back of the stands. This hotel was a present to the Turf Club who run the Curragh, enabling them room to build and develop. You know you're around serious dosh when hotels become presents.

The Turf Club believes the new stands will be a flagship for the sport internationally. Its detractors argue that the money should be put towards even better prize funds, and mutter darkly that a facility catering for up to 60,000 people is a bit of a white elephant when the record Derby crowd is just over half that. That, in turn, makes the enthusiasts get all *Fields of Dreams*, with ghostly whispers being carried on the rain as it lashes against the senior steward's box, 'If you build it, they will come.'

What no one here doubts, however, is that racing is entitled to the cash. In this uniquely incestuous world of business, sport and social status, even the very idea that there might be other avenues for this level of investment to go down hardly registers. Awash with money and success, there is also the unblinking surety that the shampoo ad is right – we're worth it. It's that confidence, rather than any clapped-out political ideals, which gets on the nerves of a lot of people peering in because even those slap-bang in the middle of the racing tent must know, deep down, that the game's success right now is built on the sort of state subsidisation that would do a Politburo proud.

At least the current system has the virtue of simplicity: the government takes all the tax that's collected from off-course bookmaker shops and gives it back to racing, and, if it comes up short of the target amount, the state picks up the balance. But since Irish racing generates only 10 per cent of bookie-shop turnover, you can see the problem for those who like to present the game here as some sort of thriving business. In fact, if it was a business, there would be a lot of letters written in scarlet-red ink winging through the door.

The obvious question as to why the government supports the industry can evoke any number of answers: employment in rural areas is one of the more familiar ones. In fact, to hear some people, it seems that the horsemen of Ireland leave their yurts on a Monday, ride out onto the vast steppes of Tipperary and Kildare and return home on Friday having spent a week living off the land in a bucolic state of grace – no mobile phones and sat. nav. in those tax-deductible Pajeros for our flowers of rural manhood.

But, in reality, racing gets this sort of subsidy because it has the political clout to get it. Which is fair enough, in its way –

after all, expecting a sector to have such pull and not use it is naïve in the extreme.

Sure, there are any number of areas where €50 or €60 million a year would alter things hugely for any number of deserving people but, as anyone who has ever been left to the tender mercies of the healing professions knows, public money tends to get swallowed up by interest groups anyway. Why pour it into the pursuit of one horse passing a red lollipop ahead of another? A lot of horsey folk might display braying arrogance but there's not much anyone can do about that. Even the Dalai Lama probably secretly believes somewhere in his heart that he really is the centre of the universe. And at least those of us having a bet get the benefit of shouting at a better standard of nag.

So, hoozah for us all!

Running total: + €1,400

Eddie G.'s Cool Too

16 July

On the basis that knowing as much as possible about the enemy can only be good, a recce into hostile territory yields a couple of hours' interrogation time with one of the Mr Bigs of the betting ring.

He, too, prefers to remain anonymous, though, not because of any wish to avoid a cuddle from the Revenue Commissioners. It's simply that, rather than floating his boat, the idea of publicity sends a torpedo spinning into his bow. Understated is what he likes, a fact emphasised by the tastefully low-key splendour of his home. A lot of money is required to maintain such a pad, and the lack of worry lines creasing his expensive tan suggests repayment worries aren't keeping him awake at night. In one way, it confirms an old prejudice, that the bookie always wins, but it's also reassuring to see concrete evidence that someone knows how to make this game pay.

Instead of wrinkles, his face has its usual expression of wry amusement, as if looking at the world is better done indulgently rather than belligerently. With almost forty years in the business behind him, that's an achievement in itself. Many of his colleagues have a rather more feral attitude to the tide of humanity that treks their way but, instead of taking a sardonic Bogart-style approach to business, he appears more like Edward G. Robinson's elegantly ruthless character in *The Cincinnati Kid*. The evidence of a steel-trap mind for figures is all around, but this Eddie G. manages to sheath it in more than a little humanity. After all, why else would he let a punting guerrilla like me in the front door?

The familiar drone of the attheraces channel is on in the luxurious office that is the headquarters of a multimillion-euro empire. The *Racing Post* is on a table and a sports website is lit up on a computer. It's all very familiar and yet alien at the same time. Eddie, to use the hackneyed phrase, has forgotten as much about punting and racing as I will ever know. In fact, no one's felt this out of their depth since people started jumping from the *Titanic*. Still, it's time to strike out for the nearest lifeboat.

'Is it really true that the bookmaker always wins?' I ask.

'That's very much untrue,' he replies. 'There are many days when we lose.'

'But over a year, say. You win, right?'

'Yes. Over a year, the bookmaker shouldn't lose. Otherwise, why is he in business?'

Behind the light humour and bonhomie, his thoughts do tend to end with slightly weary declarations of what he clearly feels to be the bleeding obvious. Totting up a profit and loss sheet at the end of each day must only encourage such confidence, especially when the evidence of your judgement can always be measured in black and white figures – or should that be black and red.

'Punters as a group, as an entity, can't win,' Edward G. continues, 'but certain punters can.'

The temptation to belly-flop on the ground and plead for the tools to become one of the latter takes longer to resist than it should.

'There might be twenty-five fellas in Ireland making a good living out of backing horses in the ring and laying them on the exchanges,' he says. 'Then there might be even more who think they're making money out of it.'

It doesn't take too long for certain basic principles to emerge. Since they're being made in a room that might, in itself, be worth more than most people's entire houses, it seems only prudent to take notes. The critical point everyone has to remember, apparently, is that every horse has a bet price and a lay price and the edge comes in realising in which one the value lies.

'A good punter has a judgement of racing and a judgement of odds which will tell him when to bet and when to bet big. If he feels a horse is a 7–4 shot and there's 9–4 available, then that is a good bet,' he says.

'Even if the horse loses?'

'Yes, because you have the value. And over time, if you keep betting like that, you can come out with a profit.'

'But deciding what's value and what's not is a judgement call.'

'That's correct. You have to have faith in your own judgement.'

'And what if you haven't?'

'Then I would suggest you stop.'

There's a pause while the implications of this sink in, but only a short one. After all, this man's time is, very much, money. There's also the fact that, while there is a constant temptation to chuck in the towel and make for a beach far, far away, there is another more pressing reality that includes having signed a contract to keep going until November. Pondering the deep inadequacies of a shaky betting judgement is probably not a great idea right now. So, instead, I ask about how long it takes to be able to confidently back your own judgement.

'It took me several years,' he concedes. 'When I started, the smaller bookmakers would be the first to put up prices and if there was any blooper about a horse's price, they'd be quickly swamped. The problem was that I was paying too much attention to what was happening with them and shifting my own prices as a result. But I was watching guys who didn't have a shilling to their name. What was I doing following them? I had to ask myself why I was being a sheep and playing follow-the-leader.'

That determination to stand his ground is only matched by a steadfast belief in a document that has long since been thrown into a corner in my less salubrious office.

'The best place to find winners is in the formbook,' he declares with a certainty born of a successful career at the betting coalface.

'There are some guys who'll say you can't win on form alone. They say you've got to get information.'

'If there's something worth listening to, it's usually backed up by the formbook. There are two-year-old races, for instance, where there's no form to go on and everyone keeps their eyes and ears open. But, otherwise, if it isn't in the book, I tend to ignore what I hear. But you have to know how to interpret it. A lot of it is feel. Take a look at the Oaks yesterday.'

Even a mention of the race is enough to provoke intestinal rumblings of a sort that are more normally associated with livestock. Peeping Fawn is now a classic winner. In fact, the filly I laid to lose a midweek maiden managed to beat the Epsom winner, Light Shift, by three-and-a-half lengths and did so despite circumstances conspiring against her. Kieren Fallon had a bad fall at Longchamp the day before and cried-off riding at the Curragh. At the same time, the filly also came into season, a detail relayed to the stewards who, in turn, announced it at the track. Not surprisingly, Peeping Fawn drifted in the betting, something Eddie G. watched like a hawk.

'What I know for certain is that we bookmakers make our money from laying short-priced horses. It's the risk and reward theory. If I lay an evens favourite for €1,000, I'm risking €1,000. If I lay a 5–1 shot, I'm risking €5,000 for the chance to get €1,000. Now, which is better for me? A lot of bookmakers, and an awful lot of amateur layers on the exchanges, don't fancy a horse, feel it can't win, and then put up any price next to it. That's crazy. Every horse has a lay price and a bet price. It all comes down to what stage you're prepared to risk. Peeping Fawn yesterday should have been an evens favourite but then came the news she was in season and she went right out to 4–1. Now, I and a lot of other people know that some horses run badly when they're in season – and some don't. So there was a situation there where you had to decide if the risk of backing her was worth it.'

'Did you lay her for much?'

'We were deliberately under the odds at all stages with her. She is very good.'

It probably isn't a great idea to regale Edward with my own Peeping Fawn experience. If there's one thing that's coming across crystal clear it is that he despises amateur bookmakers, almost as much as he distrusts the betting exchanges.

'When I'm standing on my box, who has a bet is often more important than how much they're betting. If, for instance, John Oxx, who never gambles, comes up to me and has €100 on, I'll know it's time to sell up. But the exchanges are faceless. Who is doing the laying? Are they people in the know or, for the want of a better phrase, mugs? If there are amateurs out there doing nothing but laying horses on the exchanges, then they will get cleaned out. I know it is a theoretical argument but if you want business on the exchanges, you have to be best price all the time, and I wonder will there be replacement layers out there when the first lot are cleaned out,' Eddie argues.

To which the likes of Betfair and Betdaq will no doubt reply, 'Well, he would say that, wouldn't he?' But there's no questioning the man's longevity in the business and there's little point even pretending to pose as a punting equal. It's time to gather the crumbs of wisdom gleaned over almost forty years.

'Only bet when you think there's value. So many people follow the hype. It's the old story – "This is a certainty, any price is a good price" – and you end up betting 4–5 about a 7–4 chance.

'The other thing is that it's easier to punt on jump racing rather than the flat. People believe they're taking more of a risk over the jumps so they expect a better price to compensate for the dangers. But the reality is that in conditions races especially, the better horses are the better jumpers. So, instead, of being an obstacle, the fences are actually a plus because you're getting a bigger price. There's also the fact that there's more time to recover from a mistake. On the flat, the jockey can make one wrong decision, get into a pocket and the race is over. That's just as likely as a tip up in a novice chase,' he says.

Having blown my presumption out of the water, Eddie G. proceeds to a debate about the theory of bookmaking that is hopelessly one-sided. It doesn't take long before he twigs he's talking to himself. Maybe it's my doleful face, but he thankfully brings the discussion back to a less esoteric level. Even an hour is enough to reveal that this man lives in a world so calculating, it makes my attempts to play the shrewdie seem embarrassing. Far from getting to know the enemy, this feels like peeping over the parapet, seeing Panzer Group A bearing down and recognising the bowel-dissolving certainty of being hopelessly outgunned. It's time to run away, but not before asking one question that has always nagged.

'You don't need to stand on a box anymore. But you still

do it. Out in the rain in some place a hundred miles away. Why?'

'What else would I do? And I enjoy it.'

'What part especially – besides the obvious one of winning?'

'It's an intellectual challenge,' he decides. 'People like to be proved right. You get it in the paper, going on the record, and punters get it by betting. Even the biggest and wealthiest owners will have a relatively small bet in a race, purely to add some flavour.'

'And they win, right?'

'Not always. After all, I wouldn't be here if they did. You're going to Galway, I presume.'

'Yeah, you?'

'Of course. You can't miss Galway. It'll be a good chance for you there.'

'Really?'

'There will be great value for anyone punting selectively. Don't be some lemming following the money. There'll be the usual gambles and horses going off at ridiculously short prices, but that means there'll be inflated prices on the others. You just have to find that value, no €4,000 to €2,000 bets. Slow and steady is what you want. There'll be some great each way value in some of those sixteen-plus runner handicaps.'

'I hate betting each way.'

'I would get over that, if I were you. Each way is where I lose. I'll see you at Ballybrit.'

Running total: + €1,140

Saigon Crypto and the
Stiff Upper Lip

30 July

Be it Kentucky for the Derby, Paris for the Arc or Melbourne for the Cup, the major crowds turn up for the best quality racing. It's like anything else in the entertainment game – the big gigs produce the big numbers. In Ireland, however, things are different because, in Ireland, we have Galway.

Normal criteria simply don't apply here. Instead, in their place is a self-perpetuating myth that bankrolls an industry while, at the same time, providing it with a crucially different sense of itself. If there is an essence to racing in Ireland, then it is to be found in Galway.

By all the usual commercial rules, this seven-day festival shouldn't work. The product isn't the best – in fact, much of the racing is downright mediocre. It also takes place on a track that would horrify sophisticated European turfistes and have American fans wondering what an undulating and uneven green fairground ride is doing in the middle of a racetrack. Lurking behind those deceptive appearances, however, are the cold commercial figures of a mammoth success story.

Over €30 million will be bet on the track this week. That's almost 15 per cent of betting turnover for the entire year in Ireland. In each race, up to €750,000 will be generated by moderate animals, some of whom will end up moving just as quickly around the inside of a tin can as they will around these idiosyncratic hills and hollows. Then, there are mind-boggling attendance levels. The 52,000 people that crammed in here on the fourth day of the festival in 2005 made an attendance record in Ireland. The guts of 250,000 people will be here over this week. That's 5 per cent of the country's entire population, heading west on the back of mostly rubbish horses and spending like heroes.

Purists tend to get the hump about that. In just over a month's time, the Champion Stakes will be run at Leopardstown, a Group 1 event with the cream of European bloodstock already on its roll of honour and officially rated in the world's top ten races, but there won't be 8,000 people there to watch it. That can cause weeping and gnashing among aficionados, but what the head has to get round is that the usual commercial rules are as redundant during Galway race week as the licensing laws. In fact, for seven days at the height of every summer, the word 'usual' is best left parked on the outskirts of the city, a safe distance away from Galway's determination to dissolve itself into a playfully hedonistic puddle.

Why this should be the case is something that provokes a lot of newspaper coverage which, in turn, keeps the Galway myth chugging along nicely. It's now the primary social event of the summer in Ireland. Except, this time, there is one visitor to Galway who isn't welcome and might just threaten to spoil the mood – certainly it's all that the radio stations can talk about on the long drive across the country.

Cryptosporidium is a bacteria that has taken up residence in the local water supply. According to some more excitable reports, one sip of infected water has the potential to have you sprinting for the toilet in milliseconds. The result of its visit to the west is a ban on drinking tap water and the sort of aqua minerale sales that send Perrier executives into early retirement to Monte Carlo. There is an initial curiosity value in brushing your teeth with the purest of pure Dolomite spring water, but that quickly pales when facing a shower. A long, luxuriant soaper isn't really on when you have to seriously consider the idea of a band aid over your puckered puss. Living like this for months must be almost as much of a pain in the ass as the crypto itself.

However, apart from the danger of being flushed into Lough Corrib, there literally isn't a cloud in the sky. That's the first result of the week since, overall, July has been a sodden nightmare. Having midsummer meetings abandoned because of waterlogging is the sort of phenomenon that provokes dire apocalyptic warnings from global warming experts and throws any idea of form out with the floodwater. Somehow,

Galway has timed it so that the sun emerges just in time to produce going that almost verges on perfect. It's an omen, and it's enough to make even the most arid soul look forward to the week with a shiver of anticipation.

Hours before it kicks off, the first of the choppers appear on the horizon. There was a time when beating the traffic required a certain ingenuity. Years ago, my pal's only visit to Galway included posing as a cabinet minister in the back of his uncle's Mercedes. Even then, the link between the races and politics was enough to have every branch of officialdom waving them through, despite the sort of driving that would have done credit to the Red Ball Express. But now, if you want flash, the only way to travel to Ballybrit is by helicopter.

It's not just the J.P. McManuses or Michael Smurfits of this world who do it either. A recent EU survey showed that Ireland has more privately owned choppers per capita than anywhere else in Europe. And, even if you don't own one, there's always the hire option – €300 gets you a five-minute taxi to and from the races and the frisson of being able to glance pityingly downwards on those of us roughing it on the roads. The story of how one woman took a taxi from her hotel less than a mile from the course in order to get on a chopper ten miles away and then land in the infield is already attaining mythical status.

Sure enough, half an hour before the first race the skies overhead look like something out of Saigon. Just seconds separate the landing and take off of each chopper, which make for the city as if the Viet Cong below are pointing SAM missiles. A deafening din accompanies each landing, but it's nothing compared to the sound of an economy in overdrive.

Be they billionaires, politicos, charlatans or wannabes, the end result is a raucous, heaving tide of humanity on the side of a hill which, when you think about it, represents a hell of a lot that's good about this country. Not surprisingly, for a large group of people who are at a race meeting during the middle of the week, there is a determination to tie one on that mostly transmits itself through the consumption of colossal amounts of alcohol. So, without wishing to get all misty green about it, there is something kind of cool about seeing 50,000 pissed-up punters managing to squeeze into the same space and not eat each other alive. Anyone who has ever picked their way through the remnants of a day at Cheltenham or Ascot will know the alternative, that latent stench of potential aggro that always seems ready to kick off into something a lot more serious. There are probably plenty of sociological reasons why that, apparently, isn't the case in Galway, but an easier explanation is probably to do with the absence of space to swing anything.

It would be wrong to suggest that all sections of society are represented at Galway. For one thing, the crowds are almost uniformly a shade of white-pink and the sheer open-air heartiness of it all wouldn't appeal to a lot of people, whatever their skin colour. But that still leaves a hell of a lot to work with. Overseas journalists invariably point to the determined egalitarianism of the place. The famously dry-witted former MP Clement Freud once memorably found himself in the queue for the Tote and only after a few minutes did he blinkingly realise the man in front of him was the then-Taoiseach, Albert Reynolds. Not unsurprisingly, he tried to imagine meeting a British PM under similar circumstances and failed.

That sort of informality has been ascribed to a lack of snobbery in Irish racing, but that's just wishful thinking. Snobbery is as alive and well in Ireland as anywhere else, it's just not kitted out in formal wear and a top hat. Instead, it deliberately blends into that egalitarian streak where it can nod and wink under cover of informality. Murder and rape may be terrible but God help the Irishman who is accused by his own of getting above himself.

Of course, there is always an exception to any rule and, in Galway, that exception is the long Buddha himself. Even in the days when Galway was regarded as a glorified flapper meeting on the side of a hill, Dermot Weld made the festival a target. Now that everybody else has cottoned on, he is still not so much an uncrowned king around here as a major deity. He has been the top trainer for as long as anyone can remember. Which is probably why, twenty minutes before the first race, yours truly finds out how sweaty it can be when hundreds of eyes decide you are the luckiest sonofabitch in the world.

DK is at the sort of loose end that even makes talking to a hack an option. Maybe it's an overactive imagination, but the normal din outside the weigh room seems to drop a couple of decibels. The man himself is either oblivious of this or has just become used to being the focus of so much attention that it doesn't matter any more. To those of us toddling along in cosy anonymity, however, it's enough to provoke more than a little shuffle of unease.

The jealously is understandable, though, as Weld provides the odds-on favourite in the first and he has the hot favourite for the third, a two-year-old maiden that has won a staggering seventeen times in the past. In that horribly lazy phrase that we hacks use far too often, Weld's maiden runner is known as the financial 'tank' for the week. There are people out there who would fall like leopards on this chance to figure out what the real story with Domestic Fund is. Duty demands the question be popped. The wonder is that DK plays ball.

'I'd like the ground to dry out a little more,' he states up front. 'He's quite a light-framed horse, so I wouldn't want it too testing. But he's pretty good.'

The last part is delivered with that slight nod and a purse of the lips. Normally, that would be enough to have seasoned Weld watchers sprinting for a bookie, except DK isn't finished.

'The Bolger horse is fancied a lot, I believe,' he adds.

The Bolger horse is called Chun Tosaigh and he made his debut in a Group 3 and didn't disgrace himself in it. How two-year-olds react to their first outing is never straight-forward but this one has obviously gone the right way. It's undoubtedly significant.

A good hour concentrating on the race yesterday resulted in my boiling it down to a choice between Domestic Fund and the Ballydoyle colt Lucifer Sam. He was just behind Weld's horse when they both ran in that memorable race behind Lisvale. Crucially, though, Lucifer Sam has run again and there was plenty to like about the way he had obviously improved to chase home a horse called New Approach, who has since won a Group 3. There was enough, in fact, to justify offering a nap in the paper this morning and the provision of €200 in cash to back him now. After all, it's Galway. Weld could throw anything into a race here and it would start favourite – which means the value must be elsewhere. There might even be some 2–1 floating about but if Bolger's horse is fancied, then he comes right into it too – he is New Approach's stable companion after all. But it doesn't finish there.

We're joined by a third-party so knowledgeable in the ways of the Kevin Prendergast stable that he knows what shade of underwear the trainer favours. He insists that Houston Dynimo will trump the lot of them, never mind that he finished even farther behind in the Lisvale race.

'He's been bombing since. Come on heaps. He's working with this thing that's a bloody good lead horse and he's pissing past him every morning,' he informs us.

It's an eight-runner race and I've really good word for three horses, and none of them is the one that I fancied so strongly just an hour ago. It's enough to make Billy Graham start doubting.

The festival duly kicks off with Weld's opening odds-on favourite getting chinned, which doesn't stop the faithful piling into Domestic Fund like Dunkirk evacuees climbing into a boat. He winds up an 11–8 favourite. There's also a lot of support for Chun Tosaigh and Houston Dynimo, while Lucifer Sam, in contrast, slides in the betting, and then slides a little more. It's not a good sign. I bolster myself with the knowledge that there will be less-competitive maidens than this during the week and, anyway, Fallon has been riding terribly lately. The €200 stays where it is.

The inevitability of what happens next is galling. Out in front, the fancied trio slug it out to the start of the long climb up the hill. Chun Tosaigh is the first to crack and although

Houston Dynimo keeps going well enough, Domestic Fund always looks to be holding him. And then Fallon comes sailing up the outside to edge the favourite by a head. Lucifer Sam ends up a 3–1 winner. It's as good an example as any of too much information being a curse.

Winner number one of the week for Weld comes in the next race, the amateur feature, which sees the unheralded 12–1 shot, Loyal Focus, win by nine long-looking lengths. It's a race that Weld likes to win because, aged sixteen, it gave him his very first winner as an amateur jockey when Ticonderoga was successful. That's a nice hook for us hacks to get stuck into when writing about the day but, from a betting point of view, it's irrelevant. Domestic Fund was the one for Weld followers tonight, not Loyal Focus. Still, it's a long week.

Running total: + €1,060

Bertie's Black Beauty Boob

2 August

There's another thing that's different about Galway. Anywhere else, the most coveted spot on a racecourse is the winner's enclosure. Believe the hype here and the holy of holies is a nondescript tent at the back of the grandstand. Because, however much race fans might believe the festival is about betting and drinking, for the rest of the country, the first thing that comes to mind when Galway is mentioned is the gathering of the tribe at the famous Fianna Fáil tepee.

The fundraising that Ireland's largest political party does during race week has reached mythical status. In fact, if you listen to what their rivals make of what goes on there, then a Bacchanalian orgy of mass back-scratching, palm-greasing and bag-emptying takes place in a dimly lit, carpet-draped den of iniquity in which raddled houris would feel quite at home.

According to legend, the fate of modern Ireland has been carved up in this place. All through the years of opportunity that the Celtic Tiger provided, there were platoons of property developers, or builders as they were known in poorer times, apparently queuing up to get into the tent with their best bib and tucker on, chequebooks at the ready. In the subsequent tribunals that have examined the links between government and big business, the races kept cropping up with a regularity that had the sceptics nodding in a manner that suggested they knew all along. The result is that this tent is now more synonymous with Galway than Dermot Weld.

A hardy phalanx of news reporters is scouting the pow-wow, like cavalry tailing well-togged-out injuns. For these boys and girls, the races might as well be taking place on the moon. Their only objective is to tail as many celebs as possible with the No. 1 celeb undoubtedly being Bertie Ahern. It is surely no coincidence that the Soldiers of Destiny congregate at this event. If, for instance, such a bash was held on a classic day at the Curragh, it would look far too elitist, especially for a prime minister whose persona is so ordinary he could be called Joe. But the whole egalitarian vibe of Galway is, as Bertie might say, gift. Everyone else comes here – why not us?

Sure enough, after the big race Der Taoiseach ventures from the wigwam and mooches among his people in the parade ring. Pressing a bit of flesh here and there, he manages to convey the impression that he has no idea that his every move and utterance are being recorded by the scrum of photographers and reporters buzzing around him like bees. There is a tantalising moment, however, when a pair of glamour models from a tabloid newspaper are steered towards the eye of the storm and a vision of the following day's headlines flashes before everyone's eyes – 'Bertie's Boob' or 'Guess Who Bertie's Backing?' There can be no more than 170 pounds weight between the two girls, and 100 of that is bosom. The Big Chief is pointed away just in time.

No doubt, some overseas racing enthusiasts will look at a PM wandering about such an environment and ponder the special relationship that must exist between racing and the Irish establishment. However, since Bertie would happily attend the opening of an envelope, that's reading far too much into it. Be it a race meeting, football match or funeral, our leader will be there, as long as it is in his interests to be there.

A speculative visit to the famous tent itself results in a similarly underwhelming conclusion. There are a few large, shaven-headed men in XXXL shirts standing guard at the entrance to the 'corporate section' but there is nothing to distinguish any one of the white marquees from the other. There's certainly no Caesar's Palace razzmatazz on the outside of the fastest fundraiser in the west. In fact, inside, it could be a well-to-do wedding, apart from the Tote terminals dotted around, and a tangible air of determination that everyone's going to have a good time, no matter what. With a place at one of the fifty or so tables costing €400 – and there are ten places at each table – that's hardly a surprise. Apparently, though, the golden days of the tent are over: it's a victim of its own fame. There might be a full house today but for most of these punters, €400 is a bit of a stretch. Today, real money doesn't want to be seen here. Instead, it has the option of the new €22 million Killanin Stand where any wheeling and dealing can be done in private boxes – even at Galway, some people are more equal than others.

Funnily enough, the parade ring is one of those places where the divide narrows rather than widens. As usual, those who really want to get in appear to have no problem doing so: as well as millionaire owners and racing royalty, a steady flow of people with no connection to anyone or anything running in the race meanders through. The usual motive is to secure a good position for watching the big screen that's perched on top of the weigh room. During a race, anyone looking out from the weigh room has a view of hundreds of faces staring intently a few metres above their heads. It's a curiously religious sensation, especially when the faithful start swearing at whatever favourite is starting to struggle. By Day Four, visions of desperately imploring faces grimacing at the large screen have become far too common to mean anything else but good news for the bookies.

Thanks to DK's runner, Princely Hero, in the last race on Wednesday, however, things are just about even on the betting score in my little corner of the parade ring. In fact, standing in that little corner has paid off very nicely, thank you. The mile maiden last night contained a number of runners who would probably find it difficult to get out of the way of a stationary train – we are talking about a really bad race. Of those with any sort of form, it was the regally bred De La Grandera who stood out. In terms of looks, he stood out even more. It might have been Victor Mature prancing around before the race, such was the toned sleekness of De La

Grandera's massive chest except, like Victor, there is a strong suspicion that behind the swagger lies not very much at all. The others are so uninspiring, though, that a bandwagon develops.

A staggering €620,000 is bet with the on-course bookmakers alone on this race. Most of it is on the favourite who ends up possibly the best backed odds-on shot of the week. It's moments like this that test a punter's resolution. De La Grandera is a thief just waiting to put on a mask. Every instinct screams he will chuck it in once he claps eyes on that hill. But is that doubt enough to pile into something else? As the horses canter down to the start, an agony of indecision is finally resolved when DK winds up standing alongside me again.

'There's a hole in this favourite, you know,' he declares idly. 'I wouldn't know how much heart is there.'

'Really?' is the slightly hoarse reply. 'Which leaves your horse as the one to beat then, right?'

'One would think so,' the great man grins and sidles off to Princely Hero's owner nearby.

They're loading up as, somewhat frantically, I push into the mêlée in the betting ring and, through judicious use of the elbow, secure a tasty €700 to €200.

Sure enough, De La Grandera and Fallon go into an easy lead but it's almost possible to hear the doubts entering our Victor's noggin as he starts the final mile climb to the finish. There is enough of a gradient at Galway to test even the bravest animal, but, for this one, there's no debate at all. He downs tools faster than a navvy at lunchtime.

Instead of the favourite, it's a creature called Mojito Royale who stretches Princely Hero almost to breaking point but, crucially, Princely Hero has a head to spare on the line.

Galway might last for seven days but four is about the limit for anyone even semi-concerned about their liver. The modern tendency is for a younger clientele to be sent into the line for the last three days, which are part of a Bank Holiday weekend. It's a pattern that's hardly discouraged by the powers that be. It isn't difficult to picture the fresh-faced funster of today turning into the grizzled Galway veteran of tomorrow. However, those of us already grizzly enough to hang around with bears tend to view Thursday in the same way the boys in Saigon regarded the choppers.

The big hurdle, worth €210,000, is the feature event and, along with the Ladies' Day tag, it's enough to draw the largest attendance of the week at almost 47,000. Most of them manage to get the main race dead right, too, as the heavily backed favourite, Farmer Brown, dots up. As with most of the week, the flat racing is very ordinary but that doesn't stop something rather extraordinary developing in the second-last race.

The number fourteen horse rejoices under the name of Black Beauty. In thirteen starts in Britain, he won twice, but, this year, he has run a couple of times for a new trainer, John Murphy, and managed to finish only fourteenth and sixteenth. Both runs were tersely summed up on the irish-racing.com website with 'never a factor' and 'always in rear'. However, that doesn't seem to be putting people off backing him. There's some 20–1 about at first, then sixteens: the initial impression is that they're backing the jockey on board, a certain K. Fallon. In short, it looks like the sort of mug punting that bookies thrive on – except it turns into much more than that. The 16–1 disappears and then so does the 14–1 and 12–1. A speed gun is required to see the 10–1 flash past and, before we know it, even the single figures start vanishing.

The ring is a fascinating place when a real gamble develops like this. There is a noise to it, a feverish, rumbling drone which isn't a million miles away from a hunting pack that has picked up the scent. Everyone's senses seem to heighten, even those with only €5 in their hands. No one wants to be left behind when there's a potential killing to be made – especially not the bookmakers who start to scan the boards the way a fox might peep round at the horizon behind him.

This is also when any veneer of civility is tossed aside in the face of rising panic. Punters want to get on and bookies want to lay off. The result is a traffic jam of humanity that makes the Mad Cow Roundabout look restrained. Delicacies are tossed away like inhibitions on an ashram. Any punters standing around risk being mown down by bookies' runners simultaneously sprinting and shouting in order to get the last of the 8–1. People crash into each other like battery-housed ninepins.

The one person apparently unfazed by it all is Eddie G. who is at the other end of the ring, staring out with that familiar indulgent smile. Not a bead of perspiration dots his expensively burnished forehead. He probably wouldn't sweat running for an air-raid shelter. But this is the kind of scenario that might provoke one of his rare bets. As he repeated over and over again, value is the key. Whatever value there might have been in Black Beauty has long since disappeared which must leave others in the race at longer prices than they should be, and the horse that provoked this expedition to an open-air sauna in the first place is now the sort of price that he really shouldn't be at all.

My focus switches to Shayrazan who, a couple of days ago, ran in a seven-furlong handicap here. At first glance, he had a far from clear run when stuck on the inside but that can happen sometimes, all dressed up and nowhere to go. In this case, it happened quite a long way from the finish and his jockey, Christy Geoghegan, accepted the game was up, allowing the horse to come home in his own time. Watching the rerun immediately afterwards on the big screen was enough to provoke an internet search for the horse's form. One run stood out, a fine effort when just out of the money in last year's Mile, the feature on the second day. Course form is always a plus around Galway because not every horse relishes the rough and tumble of the place. Another plus for this horse is the trainer, James Leavy. He is no household name but he's also no mug. He has won at the festival before and his horses have a tendency to run big races at big prices. Shayrazan's a much longer price now than he should be. He was 12–1 a couple of days ago but there's twenties all round the place now. With the extra furlong in his favour, this might be a bet – an each way bet of the sort that Eddie G. likes.

There've been a couple of each ways already this week. The first, Brenin, a 20–1 shot on Monday, ran nowhere, the second, another 20–1 merchant called Strike An Ark, ran just outside the placings. Brenin was more fun. There's something dreadfully antiseptic about betting each way. That's an irrational prejudice of course but, still, it just feels way too calculating. Since betting is about little else except calculation, that's a bit of a problem – but so too is losing both ways.

There are bits of 25–1 floating around about Shayrazan – and that seems way too big. He's even got an inside draw on the rail. This horse must have a serious chance. Maybe it's the atmosphere of wholesale greed all around but €100 each way suddenly turns into €200 on the nose. Even when I get the ticket, it takes an effort not to hand it back and plead a mistake. Anywhere else and this might have happened but, at Galway, with a mob that has the scent of a monster gamble in its nostrils, there are no niceties, so it's Shayrazan in a big way.

Not once does Black Beauty threaten to outdo his literary namesake in terms of a happy ending. It would need ten Fallons at the peak of their powers to get him anywhere near and, eventually, he winds up twelfth. Of the €620,000 bet with the bookmakers on this race alone, almost half of it remains in their bags, thanks to Black Beauty: just another typical Galway gamble gone pear-shaped. Not that it matters to those of us who have looked elsewhere.

Seamus Heffernan had Shayrazan well back on the rail in a similar position to the one the horse was in forty-eight hours ago but, this time, Heffernan manages to get him off the rail as they run down into the dip. This gives him options. He can go left, right or up the middle. The safe option is to steer to the outside, but that means giving away valuable ground. The percentage play is to stay put and hope for a gap. The high-risk strategy is to head back to the rail. Heffernan does just that.

It looks hopeless. A line of horses are slugging it out in front of him, including the leader, Peculiar Prince, who is ridden by Shayrazan's old pal, Christy Geoghegan. He is all out, driving for everything with his whip in his right hand.

The pressure momentarily causes Peculiar Prince to come off the rail. Heffernan is into the gap like a bullet. Shayrazan proves there's nothing wrong with his courage and sticks his chestnut neck out like a hero. At the line, he is half-a-length in front.

Understandably, the congregation around the parade ring doesn't exactly raise the roof. The winner's returned at 20–1, after all, and I'm too stupefied to say anything. In fact, only the horses returning to unsaddle is enough to provoke movement. It has worked out perfectly.

The horse ran his guts out and the jockey was nothing short of inspired. Through sheer stubbornness, I had double the original stake on the nose – that's €5,000. It's unbelievable. Just a pity, then, it wasn't €200 each way.

Running total: + €6,340

A Peep at the Future

26 August

It won't stop raining. This is August and meetings are being cancelled because of waterlogging. That's simply not supposed to happen. It's bad enough living on a wet rock for most of the year but now is normally a happy time, when we surface for air and point our painfully pale faces at a watery sun without worrying about being washed overboard. Instead of which, everyone's cowering for cover.

It's throwing everything off-kilter. From a punting point of view, this really is supposed to be a happy time, when targets sail beatifically past, just waiting to be lined up and blown out of the water. Normally, there's at least a couple of months of fast-ground form to work on. Handicap good-things can run up streaks and maidens can be boiled down to an almost inevitable result. The top stuff is reassuringly constant – horses are at their peak, they've got runs under their belts and there's a consistent thread of summer ground form – except there isn't any this year, because there's too much damn *uisce* about.

Some of the results are crazier than a bag of cats. For instance, if there's one thing surer than death, it is that the Phoenix Stakes will be won by Coolmore. The past nine renewals of Europe's first Group 1 of the year for juveniles have belonged to Magnier & Co. This year, they have an unbeaten Royal Ascot winner who's already favourite for next year's Guineas. Henrythenavigator starts at 1–2 for what's expected to be a go-down-and-come-back job – except the heavy ground at the Curragh track makes getting round the Cape look like a bit of a skylark. There's a shock result when Henry gets stuffed by the 25–1 complete outsider Saoirse Abú. She's won just one of her five previous starts – only the blind or the mentally ill could have given her a hope in hell of winning.

That's not to say there aren't still chances out there.

Lisvale has the second start of his career at Tipperary in a Listed race and goes off at a remarkable 7–2. For those of us sniffing around betting offices, there is no trouble getting 4–1 in the morning. It's a remarkable price. Lisvale is a winner of one of the hottest maidens all year and yet it's a Ballydoyle colt, Achill Island, beaten on his only run to date, that's the well-supported favourite. Lisvale isn't even his biggest threat, apparently. Brazilian Star beat what can only be described as glorified flotsam over the course and distance three weeks ago, but is still well backed. Sometimes, the betting market throws up chances like this and, after Lisvale hoses up, the only wonder is why there isn't more than €800 to €200 on him. The other wonder is why he's also part of an each way double with Limonia in a crap handicap at Folkestone five minutes later.

Each way doubles are my new thing. After spending a lifetime shunning the each way concept, it's now not enough to bet each way on one horse. Instead, I've managed to convince myself that doubling it up is the clever way to go. It's tough to figure out the intelligence of that when Limonia runs up the far side rail while everything else elects to run up the stands rail. Sure enough, the horse that sounds like she's named after a stain remover provokes a few stains of her own by finishing fourth.

It quickly becomes obvious that the cost of each way doubles adds up faster than even a Shayrazan boosted tank can cope with, especially when the second leg keeps infuriatingly missing out on the frame. Theoretically, the concept is perfectly reasonable: a couple of nicely priced runners with reasonable chances provide an opportunity to win big time while, at the same time, offering a comfortable, and profitable, safety net if one or both find something too good. A colleague swears by them. Hardly a day goes by without him putting down a €50 each way double on something. The losses all add up, however, when they miss the frame, especially when I've been playing €100 each way doubles – and even more especially because I've been doing one every day for a fortnight. By the time that old each way antipathy returns with a bang, considerably more than €1,000 has disappeared one way. No doubt, a cool head would advise perseverance, insisting that all you need is for one to come up in spades, but that requires patience that some of us simply don't possess.

It's at such moments of adversity that a person reverts back to their natural instincts and the same applies to punting. Getting up the odd 9–4 or 3–1 winner isn't going to send anyone sprinting towards five-figure profits, but enough of them come in to make up for the losers. After a while, it becomes obvious that, while losses aren't at the black-hole level, any profits there might be aren't going to fund a major lifestyle change either. It all feels like things have stalled at that running-hard-to-stand-still stage again.

There's no doubt that the appalling weather isn't helping things. Maybe by now the deep-ground conditions should be throwing up a form consistency of their own, but it doesn't work like that. Everybody wants to run their horses and it's only human nature to run them when they're fit and ready, even if every other instinct is telling you to wait for decent going. Who knows how many wheels will be working on the bus by the time you get any of that, so the result is races where many of the runners resemble troops picking their way through a muddy minefield.

Today, this litany of soggy mayhem makes the opening of the new Dundalk racecourse all the more significant. Ireland's first all-weather track has a surface that's reassuringly standard with no requirement to indulge in the linguistic interpretation of yielding to soft as distinct from plain yielding. Fourteen years of planning and €38 million – over €11 million of which is a government grant – has been ploughed into the new racecourse. It is modelled on New York's Belmont Park and, although it's got only a tenth of that famous track's crowd capacity, the fact it's here at all is an achievement in itself.

The internecine squabbling of various interest groups meant that, for a long time, a lot of people felt we could rub along quite happily without an all-weather and, even if we couldn't, better locations could be found than the border town where it isn't so long since hunt-the-Provo was the only available leisure pursuit. But, despite everything, it's now here and looking pretty spick and span too.

There's no doubt that the lowly trudge of most of the all-weather racing in Britain, where bad horses run for bad prize money in order to provide a product for those bad off-course bookmakers, turned a lot of people off the idea of a similar track here. Watching Southwell or Wolverhampton can feel like a life sentence sometimes. There are beasts winning on these courses that make you reach for the Trade Descriptions Act when the word 'racehorse' is used. Rubbish will always beat worse, but it's very rubbishy indeed when creatures that could be housed in kennels end up winning.

Another reason for queasiness among some is the very standardisation that all-weather racing provides. One of Irish racing's great selling points has always been its diversity. This smacks of month-long stays in samey midwestern dust buckets with names like Prairie Dog Downs and Hillbilly Fields.

Today, however, there is no hint of unease present. Normally, the pattern for such openings is a grim determination among the powers-that-be to paint a picture of how everything that sails in Irish racing waters is pristinely perfect

– official reaction to any coverage that doesn't bring to mind Divine Brown and a Dyson is invariably poor. This time, though, even the sceptics have to acknowledge that the PR bumph looks to have a point. Everybody is clambering to get inside the all-weather tent, and anyone outside is destined for a cold, wet and solitary stay. So much is blatantly obvious when John Oxx starts waxing lyrical about the new track.

Oxx is a top man, the go-to trainer when a hack needs a realistic assessment of something in the game. Not that he's a rent-a-quote merchant. In fact, the man labelled 'honest John' by his colleagues would much rather the phone didn't ring at all. It's just that when it does, he finds it impossible not to behave in the sort of civilly decent manner that some of his more excitable brethren quite often find hard to muster. The downside of that behaviour is that the damn calls keep coming. But if there is one thing John Oxx can manage besides training top-class thoroughbreds, it is maintaining a perspective on the real world.

This isn't as easy as you might think. There are some in the training ranks whose radar fails to extend beyond their own wallets and a drainpipe-narrow sense of self-interest. The pressures of remaining competitive in a tough business means there is often little time to look up. Oxx, on the other hand, is possessed of an obvious intelligence, an impressive articulacy and the self-confidence to push neither. He is also a man with a keen sense of racing's tradition, and a list of owners that includes similar men, such as the Aga Khan. So, it isn't a huge leap of the imagination to picture Oxx as someone who might view the new course with a blearier eye than most. Such presumption, however, gets blown out of the all-pervasive water.

Phrases such as 'the future' and 'hugely significant,' as well as mention 'no negative about it' tumble from the man's mouth about this new all-weather heaven. From a lot of people, such enthusiasm would require half-a-hundred-weight of salt to make it palatable. But, to hear Oxx talk it up means the Dundalk authorities must be on to a winner. And, typically, there's a line of logic running through what he says that makes you think he might, indeed, have a point about the future.

Even in America, there is a rapid switch from the traditional and unforgiving dirt tracks that take a horrible toll of injuries each year to the new polytrack surface. Major courses, such as Del Mar and Arlington, have already torn up their old dirt and replaced it with a synthetic substitute that has dramatically cut injury rates. Plenty are complaining that old dirt form simply doesn't translate to polytrack, and that it encourages a different, more patient kind of racing, but that hasn't stopped the switch. In fact, within a decade, the breeding of specialist dirt horses could be a thing of the past. If that happens, we could be peering into a brave new world of true international competition, which will be good news for this side of the pond.

If John Oxx says it is easier for a turf horse to translate its form to polytrack than a dirt horse, then the best bet of the year is that that's the case. Take that to its logical next step and the level playing field that European trainers have wanted for years in terms of travelling to the Breeders' Cup may be just around the corner. Except it won't be a field, it will be a gooey, sticky surface of recycled rubber and wax.

'It could go all over the world,' Oxx says. 'Australia, for instance, would look to be ideal for it.'

This, remember, is a man who has trained champions like Sinndar, Azamour and Ridgewood Pearl, and he waited until their careers were over before reaching for plaudits that even then were little pearls of understatement.

'Are we talking the future here, John?'

'We could be.'

As pictures go, that's a pretty big one: years of racing tradition on different continents changing forever.

Perhaps it's hardly surprising. The world is getting smaller every minute in so many ways, why not in this? Now, finally, Ireland has its own little glimpse of that future. A little late maybe, but still, right here, under the mournful shadow of the Cooley Mountains.

That's the big picture. The little one is trying to get a handle on who's going to win today.

It's remarkable how little ideas and impressions can come back in this game. The consensus might be that an all-weather surface demands speed from the front, but a mental image from all of seventeen years ago encourages the view that it might be good old stamina that ends up the vital element around here. Raw speed is, of course, a vital element to any racehorse, but it's not the only one.

For instance, in 1990, Ibn Bey had a lot of things going for him but speed wasn't one of them. Yet, it still took an outstanding American champion in Unbridled to beat him in that year's Breeders' Cup Classic. The details are rather hazy now, but the mental picture of Ibn Bey being driven almost from the start by Richard Quinn still remains. We're talking about an Irish Leger winner here, a stayer, and yet he got within inches of winning one of the world's great races.

Subconsciously, the message got through. Speed is all very well, but the horse has got to be able to make it last.

Which is why, for most of the week, An Tadh has looked an ideal candidate for the six-furlong premier handicap. He is a horse with a lot of toe but he's a Group 3 winner at seven furlongs. It looks an ideal combination for here. And then he gets a perfect draw in stall two. Johnny Murtagh has picked him over That's Hot, another Ger Lyons hope, and it is an understatement to say the man from Meath is in a bit of form.

Murtagh is collecting Group 1s the way a squirrel gathers nuts. He's on one of those hot streaks where he can make the job look ridiculously easy. Of course, it goes without saying that Peeping Fawn has provided two of those Group 1s: the Yorkshire Oaks was an odds-on doddle but the Nassau at Goodwood saw her beat Mandesha and Light Shift. She was so impressive in that race that she is now officially rated as the best filly trained in Europe for seven years. There's no point going on about the past when faced with this sort of quality. The only consolation is that if one is to make a fool of oneself, at least there's a certain style in doing it spectacularly.

One of the nice things about a track like Dundalk is that the starts aren't so far away that hiking boots and a map are required to find them. It's also remarkable how quiet things are behind the stalls. Any idea that there's some kind of hoot-fest going on all the time between the jockeys and the stalls handlers is way off the mark. Things are much too serious for that. A few of the jocks mutter to each other but mostly it's pretty po-faced. The other noticeable thing is how few horses react badly to the stalls. It really is a remarkable act of persuasion to get a large animal to walk into such a small space and stand still for what can be a lengthy stay, but that's what most of them do.

'All in!' roars one of the stall handlers, raising a yellow flag at the same time. There isn't as much of a metallic clang as you might expect when the gates open and then the process of removing the stalls for the next race begins with the nearby tractor cranking into gear.

Unfortunately, An Tadh gets the sort of break that would be perfect in an all-out sprint: he gets out too well. Murtagh takes a grip and tries to persuade him to drop the bit but eight-and-a-half stone of jockey is no match for half-a-tonne of horse. The head-tossing struggle continues almost to the straight, by which time An Tadh's luck has burned out.

There isn't even the consolation of seeing the stamina theory come up trumps since the winner, Rainbow Rising, won over five furlongs on his last start. Still, that's no bad thing. There doesn't look to be any obvious bias to the track: horses win from the front and come from the back. There's no greyhound-like blitz necessary to get round the bends and the surface appears to be even and fair throughout, all of which means that form should work out.

There are guys in Britain who make it their business to focus on the all-weather and bet on nothing else, and that's with a lot of bad horses. Since the most important consideration in working out any race is the ground, the uniformity of the polytrack looks like a godsend. It really could pay to watch this stuff like a hawk: just a pity, then, that it's a month until the next meeting.

Running total: + €5,405

Irish Bird Is Mad

30 August

It takes Deal Breaker just fifty-eight seconds to win the Longfield Stakes at Tipperary. Eleven of his opposition pass the post just milliseconds after him and, back at the furlong pole, the other runner in the race is about to be put out of her misery. Nos Na Geeha's phonetic spelling means 'like the wind' in Irish and, right now, the translation leaves a bitter taste.

It was just the second race of her short career. The brown filly was at the back of the field when she stumbled and sent her jockey out of the saddle. Anyone tearing their gaze away from the finish knows immediately the only thing left is the tender finality of the vet's bullet. However, most of the small crowd here on a Thursday evening barely even register the little two-year-old's death, not because of heartlessness or cruelty, but because the one absolute truth about racing is that the most important race is always the next one. Already, Nos Na Geeha is reduced to an abbreviated entry in the formbook – 'ur over 1f out; dead'. The cold, unemotional summation of a life barely lived.

The first time I saw a horse die was at a point to point. It happened at the last fence, which is always surrounded by people eager to get as close to the action as possible. The ground was only barely raceable and freezing rain had lashed the course all day. A chestnut mare, all but tailed off, splashed through the muck towards us, obviously exhausted. Her rider knew better than anyone she was knackered. It wasn't a case of some cowboy going for glory but, after racing for the most of three miles, he reckoned on finishing. The mud-caked horse would have stopped in a few strides if she was let, so the jockey threw everything into a flurry of arms and legs to force her over. She barely left the ground, crashed through the fence and stuck a front leg out on the other side to try and keep from falling.

It sounds like a gunshot when bone cracks. Sometimes, it can be as clear as a farmer shooting rabbits behind you. This was more muted, maybe because of the howling wind. Some elemental instinct stopped her from sinking into the mud with exhaustion. She made to stand properly but tottered forward for a few steps like someone pushed downstairs. The bottom of the leg that had failed to keep her up, swung disgustingly loose, free of all contact with the rest of the limb. She was trying to balance on three legs and a stub of bone.

There was some muted swearing and a few exclamations of horror from a crowd that didn't know whether to turn away or try to do something – but nothing could be done. The mare was finished. One glance was enough to know that, except looking away again was impossible. It was all a lot of us could do not to throw up, but still we looked at the helpless animal.

She was quite calm, her flanks heaving after the effort of the race, covered in mud, the sweat rising from her back mixing in with snorting hot gasps from her nostrils which billowed upwards when meeting the cold air. But there was also bewilderment. That's the hardest thing for anyone looking at a fatally injured horse. Despite the injury and the exhaustion, she still wanted to move and a few hardened souls had to jerk harshly at the loose reins to stop her. That made the horse raise her head in protest and there was enough white in her eye to confirm that terrible incomprehension of what was happening.

There were a few shouts to clear some space which most of us obeyed gratefully. The little mare stayed mostly still for what seemed like an eternity but must have been only a minute. Then a Land Rover pulled up and the vet got out. It didn't take long.

By now a smaller group of people, presumably those connected with the horse, had gathered round. One woman gently rubbed the horse's nose while the vet got ready. There were no tears. In fact, there was no visible emotion at all, which, of course, didn't mean there wasn't any. Nothing mattered except ending this as soon as possible, for everyone's sake, especially the horse. A black pistol containing a 0.32

bullet suddenly appeared. The target corresponds to a spot in the middle if lines are drawn between the left eye and the right ear and from the right eye to the left ear. It demands a steady hand and a steadier nerve. No one wants to have to use a second bullet. The vet brought his arm up quickly and the shot rang out, sending crows squawking from nearby trees. There was no need for a second shot. A few reflex shudders and it was over.

For someone who had only seen serious injuries on television, where the cameras swing away from the stricken animal politely hidden behind the big green canvas screens, it was a pretty shattering experience. For some reason, no one seemed to know the mare's name. The rain seemed to have reduced everyone's token paper race sheet to mush and the few people I spoke to didn't know either. A battered horse box ended up parked next to the sad anonymous carcass that lay pathetically by the last fence as we left to go home, already ignored and forgotten.

Except the mental image keeps coming back, usually among large groups of punters shouting their choice home. Gathered around a TV in a bookies' shop, it's impossible sometimes not to look at the action on the racetrack as a visual product consisting only of the money that's been invested in it. The cheers that go up when a danger comes crashing down at the last are not malevolent, just simply ignorant of what that antiseptic picture on screen really means for flesh, bone and spirit.

Anyone who has worked with horses, for even a short while, knows differently. Now, the danger when venturing into this territory is to get all anthropomorphic about it, which is a fancy way of saying that animals ain't humans. However, even the most fleeting contact with horses confirms they are individuals. A season spent working at a stud farm many years ago was long enough to realise that.

If there wasn't individuality involved, there wouldn't have been a rush to get to certain mares and their foals in the morning as we led them out to the paddocks. In particular, there was always a sprint to get to Tranchard, a big chestnut mare with the sort of laid-back manner that her son inherited in spades. We could have eaten our breakfast off his back. On the long walk to the fields, there was barely a need to put a protective hand on his shoulder as he loped alongside his mother. In fact, if Tranchard Junior had barked, we'd have taken him home and parked him in front of the fire. Others were very different, including, typically, the most valuable one of all.

We are talking of a time so long ago that the farm of memory is now a series of colossal housing estates on the outskirts of Dublin. Back in 1989, Airlie Stud was possibly the number two stud operation in the country and its star was a tall, dark goldmine called Irish Bird. Possessed of only moderate racing talent herself, some genetic fluke meant she couldn't stop throwing up champion offspring: Bikala won a French Derby and Assert did the same – adding an Irish Derby and an Irish Champion Stakes for good measure. As if that wasn't enough, Eurobird was good enough to win an Irish Leger. Their mother was money on legs and only needed a pair of high heels to qualify as a total crazy bitch. Getting within ten yards of her sent that neurotic black head into the sky. She was a nightmare to have to deal with. But one of her daughters made her seem like an Albanian nun.

This little demon was the one us lads did not want. Bringing the horses back in from the fields meant a ruck near the gate to get closest to the quiet mares and their malleable offspring. Irish Bird could have stood in the middle with a 'pick me' sign around her neck and still have been ignored until the poor sap left with no bridle to put a lead rope through had no other option. I was the sap on the occasion when little Bird decided to do a backward flip that included clattering her head off one of the rails that lined the stud. Normally, accidents like that resulted in a chorus of piss-taking, but this time there was only silence as the little foal scrambled back to her feet. There are pagan deities on some South Sea Islands who still have to call in their tabs on the prayers offered up in the seconds it took to determine that this potential multimillion goldmine was all right: a little dazed, maybe, but nothing obvious that the head man could point at and go nuclear.

However, apart from the stresses of trying not to kill millions of pounds worth of prize horseflesh, there were moments when it was a conscious pleasure to stand at a paddock rail and watch some of the foals playing. The first tentative steps away from their mothers quickly turned into the sort of packs that any small child would recognise, all playful nipping and shouting and racing from one corner of the paddock to another. Even at that age, there was a pecking order with some foals dominating and others meekly following along. There was an established wisdom that the 'leaders' were likely to turn into the best runners, but that's crap.

One of the star youngsters of 1989 was a little colt by the

Derby winner Reference Point whose stud career at that point was still full of potential. The mare was La Mer, a champion in New Zealand, whose personality could hardly have been more different to her next-door neighbour, Irish Bird. Sure enough, the product of their short, shuddering union was a classy little operator: easy to catch, easy to deal with, a real little prince. In the paddock, however, he turned into a regular Genghis Khan. There was no question who was boss. The tough guys who'd worked on the farm for years used to look at him aiming fly kicks at the others and grin appreciatively – this was going to be the real deal.

It was some years later that the real deal showed up again, except, this time, he had a name – Sir Henry Knyvet. The original Sir Henry hung around the court of Elizabeth 1, his namesake never came close to keeping the august company he was bred for. Instead, he ended up running mostly in bumpers and hurdles races, but never won in fourteen starts. I remember him at Fairyhouse one day in a nondescript hurdle race and feeling a stab of concern in case anything might happen to the strapping bay hulk that used to be the schoolyard bully. It was irrational, of course, but nonetheless real and it brought home again the fundamental judgement call each of us makes every time we go to the races or have a bet. These creatures are created for our entertainment.

If it wasn't for racing, there wouldn't be much need for the fragile, neurotic, pea-brained animal that is the result of hundreds of years of cross-breeding. Every aspect, from breeding to selling to training, is destined for one place only, the racecourse, where we, the public, sit or stand in various degrees of comfort to watch thoroughbreds put under pressure for our pleasure. That pressure inevitably results in some horses being injured, sometimes fatally. The majority of cases happen in the jumping game but it's hardly unknown on the flat either.

While Hurricane Run was winning the 2005 Irish Derby, another Coolmore-owned colt, Gypsy King, was being put down at the farthest part of the course away from the stands. The camera caught the shattering first steps as his jockey struggled to pull up, and then they were out of sight, that instinct to gallop after the pack reduced to pathetic hobbling bewilderment before the inevitable vet's verdict. Hurricane Run passed the post just as Gypsy King was being spared any more pain – the greatest glory and the most diabolical disaster wrapped up in a couple of heartbeats.

Any pact we make with ourselves to justify the dangers we put in front of these dumb animals is hardly Faustian but, consciously or subconsciously, every racing fan does have to come up with one. Sometimes, it's a stretch. A dozen horses were killed at the Galway festival two years ago, the grim cost of a week's indulgence. One would have to be spectacularly lacking in imagination not to examine that cost and at least briefly wonder if it's worth it. Ultimately, everyone must come to their own conclusion. Clearly, all of us involved in the game, even if it's only betting a weekend yankee, have managed it, but it can be hard not to feel doubts when faced with a stricken animal whose only future is a bullet.

The hard men dismiss such things. Those who make their living from horses usually haven't the time or the inclination to indulge in what they would categorise as fluffy sentimentalism. But the world is changing, and while racing prefers to inhabit its own cosy cocoon, it will, eventually, have to face up to what the rest of world thinks about it. Dismissing the concerns of animal rights groups as flakey whining simply isn't good enough any more. If there's only a thin veneer of civilisation separating us from the animals anyway, then keeping that veneer shiny is vitally important.

How civilised it is to push racehorses to their limit is a more complicated debate than any one financially challenged punter is ever going to get a complete handle on. The consolation for those of us who enjoy the races is that there are many more worse things going on in man's uneasy relationship with the animal kingdom than little men whipping big horses. Industrial farming and production is a world away from the care and attention lavished on the average racehorse: but it is once that horse's racing career is finished, either through injury or age, that things become less certain.

There are now centres that try to retrain and re-home injured or retired thoroughbreds. But, in an industry that sees almost 12,000 foals born every year in Ireland alone, they are still only pinpricks of comfort to an uneasy conscience. An estimated 800 thoroughbreds a year are slaughtered in Ireland, either because of injury or because their owners don't want to pay for them anymore, and there's €500 for meat. That represents only 7 per cent of the total number of foals born every year, but that low figure ignores the fact that Ireland exports the majority of the stock born here.

Is that acceptable? Is it good enough? Is it right to treat these creatures that many of us regard as noble as just mere livestock when it suits us? Put basically, does people's responsibility to the animal end once its usefulness is over? That is a question that, in years to come, is likely to become more relevant to racing's image. And, in a sport where perception is everything, the answer better be good.

Running total: + €5,975

The Price of Ignoring Rita

8 September

A pal of mine is one of that rare breed of man who is irresistible to women. Today, he is married, roped, gelded and saddled like the rest of us but there was a time when evidence of his irresistibility was maddeningly abundant. Cast-offs from the table of this miniature Eros were so beautiful it was all the rest of us could do to keep our mouths closed while explaining to the latest gorgeous, tearful creature left bewildered at getting the elbow that she really could do better for herself – like, right now.

It was offensive what he was able to chuck aside. We should have hated him, but it was hard to. For one thing, *he* didn't get it either. We are not talking about a bloke of elephantine proportions here. In fact, compared to others in the group, he looked pretty ordinary – but no man has ever been successful with the ladies by believing he can persuade them into doing anything. The fairer sex always decides and, at some United Nations forum for the advancement of female kind, the vast majority of the lactating world decided that our man was the dog's. His saving grace was an ability to keep his mouth shut about his charms, which he did possibly out of consideration, but a more likely explanation is an absolute truth about the sex game which is that the more talkie, the less naughty.

However, in a rare moment of emotional incontinence brought about by two gallons of Guinness and several spliffs of polaris-like dimensions, he once divulged how bored he was with the whole thing. The rest of us might groan softly at the latest vision of loveliness that would show up on his arm but, while we gazed in open adoration, his own gaze was glazing.

'It's a fact of life, for every 100 men dreaming of being with a beautiful girl, there's at least one guy who's tired of pretending to listen to her,' he slurred.

To which, the only response could be, 'Boo-hoo.' Except, now, I've more of an idea about what he was going on about. It's irrational, and worthy of no sympathy, but this whole project is not completely dissimilar.

I know there are hundreds out there who would give their souls to be doing this betting lark but, after five-and-a-half months, it's starting to feel just a little old – so, all together now, 'Boo-Hoo.'

I'm starting to hear the attheraces channel in my sleep. A God-awful little jingle they play between segments is now coming between me and the land of nod. It's enough to make my brain feel like it needs a shave. Every day, this incessant drone in the corner delivers endless hours of betting trends, and ground reports, and expert tips and the exciting prospect of the 3.30 from Southwell – and it's all percolating in far too deeply for comfort. No one should have to listen to Matt Chapman this much.

Matt is an attheraces presenter, the one who glistens. Clearly a student of the McCririck media school, he has honed the sort of shtick that his hero would be proud of. As with McCririck, volume is everything, and if it's possible to act like a gurning loon that's just stuck his toe into an electric socket, then all the better. The difference is that this guy comes with the sort of luminous tan that makes you reach for the after-sun lotion. Looking at it is enough to make your eyes water. Clive James once famously described a young Arnold Schwarzenegger as resembling a brown condom filled with walnuts. Remove the walnuts and you have Matt.

However, he is enthusiastic – genuinely so. There's no way that mere professionalism could provoke this sort of orgasmic bellowing every day. In a way, it's something to be envied, and when the mute button is on, and Matt's buffed-up noggin swells with excitement like the rear end of a horny baboon, you would need a hard heart not to extend some grudging admiration – in short bursts only though. Prolonged exposure is enough to provoke a lunge for some baler twine.

Any weariness on my part is not, however, Matt's fault. This whole deal isn't supposed to be tiresome, and yet routine has crept into this too, like some kind of dead-eyed dry rot. No doubt, you are dabbing the tears from your eyes right now, and any scepticism is entirely understandable. Even when the Bird Man of Ballsbridge was peering into his pint and having a dark night of the soul, it all looked kind of glamorous – the sort of raddled desperation that only jaded rock stars and impossibly lucky bastards ever get to indulge in – but there is a point when familiarity really does breed contempt.

It's been possible to set the clock by what's been happening every day for the last five months – study form, maybe decide to check out morning prices, see what's happening on Betfair, remember the calamitous luck that befalls every bet on the exchanges and, on balance, decide to stick with the bookies, evenings spent watching the likes of Ballinrobe or Sligo where only Matt is capable of rising any sort of delirium for what's on offer. It is important to watch but, sometimes, it's hard. Not down-a-mine hard, obviously, but sometimes a canary in a cage would be welcome, just for a change.

It's rare that a day goes by without me placing some kind of bet. The option of ringing up to bet is always there but it's remarkable how much time is spent in actual shops.

It could be some deep, psychological need to get out of the house and engage with the rest of humanity in an attempt to step out of über-digital isolation, but it's probably just habit. It's certainly not the most efficient way of doing business. There's no regular haunt either. After all, some pasty-faced, hollow-eyed computer freak coming in every day and having €200 on might provoke suspicion, although a regular supply of success might help that little conceit along in terms of credibility.

At least it's now possible to do any betting-shop business without feeling like a lowlife. The shops are a different world to even just a few years ago. Quite a lot of that has to do with the absence of cigarette smoke. There was a time when navigating a course through your average bookie's required radar in order to get past the toxic gloom. Facilities extended as far as a stubby pencil, with a string attached, and no further. It's a different ball game now because they're mostly chain shops with a uniformity of comfort. It's possible to get a cup of tea or coffee that won't provoke a rush to the toilet – in fact, there are even toilets now. No more can the local publican's attempt at bookmaking be identified by the rising steam of the back wall urinal mating with cigarette smoke percolating out a window. When a latte is available in a bookie's, we really have come a long way.

Not that very many customers appear to care about such things, certainly not obviously. We're a weird lot, those of us who spend considerable amounts of our lives in these places. One of the oldest clichés in the game is that everyone's equal over and under the turf, which is the kind of rubbish that only those at altitude can even pretend to believe. Whatever about underground, on top, the possession of plenty of moolah makes some a helluva lot more equal than others. However, the cliché has more resonance in a main-street shop than any racecourse. It's still crap to suggest that money is anything other than all-important, but at least we all have to stand in the same room. The guy in the suit nipping out from the office for five minutes to have €50 on Tiger Woods in the Open has to rub shoulders with the Runyonesque bum making his 50¢ yankee on the computer dogs last long enough for the rain to stop outside.

Always, though, these shops have atmosphere: that blend

of optimism that this might be 'the big day' mixed with the stoical acceptance that something will come along to mess it up. It's like being a fan of the worst football team in the world. The hope that somehow things will be different this time is always fighting a losing battle against the sure knowledge that they will foul up. In such circumstances, the ability to appreciate a certain grim humour isn't so much an option as a requirement.

Betting at the track is different because everyone's so determined to be in the know – the lowest form of life here is a mug. The presence of so many men standing on boxes with large bags of money in front of them is a sure sign that such a species is hardly endangered but no one's ever going to publicly apply for mug-relief. A shrewd, knowing face must always be presented to the world – or else, what's the point?

My earlier resolve to go to the races more was genuine, but doomed. It's remarkable how real life always seems to interfere with its made-up cousin. Sitting into the car and pointing it on a four-hour drive to Tralee is not really on when two small boys are yowling for their grub – it was a nice idea, but not a runner. Such freedom is the preserve of those without responsibilities – or those with exceptionally profitable expense accounts.

The reluctance to indulge fully again on the exchanges is a different matter entirely, but that's going to have to change. The 'Big L' is a constant presence but throwing everything on to the back of fate feels like a copout. There are only two months left to get within sniffing distance of this mythical €50,000. Choosing to ignore the easiest, the most convenient and, often, the best-value option is a luxury I can no longer afford.

The problem, though, is that thinking about a renewed attack isn't exactly getting my pulse racing. Shayrazan was brilliant, but a lot of that was due to how unexpected it was. Many gambling addicts say it's not winning that's the big turn on, but rather the process of betting itself – scribbling out the docket, keying in the figures – it's the whole 'travelling expectantly' being better than the 'arriving' thing. It must be personality driven, because any buzz I used to feel when getting money down has well and truly vanished.

It's all become desperately routine, like taking the bins out on a Wednesday. €100 here and €50 there most days starts to feel like something on the daily checklist – change the baby, buy the milk, put the bet down, collect the post. On average, about one in three is a winner, the normal rate of winning favourites. One in two is what the real heavyweights manage. Overall, this success rate just about keeps things on an even keel, but that's hardly the idea. Not losing much and not winning much makes the whole thing pretty redundant.

Eddie G.'s mantra about betting the value makes sense and there are occasions when prices on certain horses are just plain wrong – Lisvale at Tipperary was a perfect example – but, as a rule, there isn't enough of a turnover to keep things ticking along at the rate that's needed. They're rare enough to require each of them to be a winner and that's just not a runner. As Eddie explained, one big-priced touch can keep the show on the road. But what I need is an off-ramp to the skies. It doesn't help that I suspect that my one big touch has probably already happened.

In any case, my suspicion that this might just be a losing battle has resulted in some bad habits returning. It is a guilty pleasure now to indulge in one of those days when the study of form is replaced by a quick look at the cards and trusting to first impressions – not to the extent of that going-through-the-card stroke from years ago, but going with the gut all the same. It's remarkable how similar the results are compared to spending hours slaving over a hot computer, especially in the maidens and conditions races that make up the bulk of turnover. Eddie G.'s insistence that each way betting in handicaps is the way to go has fallen by the wayside. That might be the bet he loses most on but it's also the kind of punting that Virg and the boys in the ring ignore – and, when it comes to choosing sides, there's no competition. The good guys might mostly end up losing but we're fighting the good fight. That is, up to a point.

If there's a guilty pleasure in cutting corners, it is like leave from the front to simply take a day off and not even think about betting. Matt the Presenter might regard it as treasonous, but to switch off attheraces and indulge in an afternoon matinée where Bob Mitchum sleep walks his way into the voluptuous bosom of Rita Hayworth is a real pleasure sometimes. The nagging voice at the back of my mind is always there but, every once in a while, it does no harm to press the mute button on him too.

What's great about this game, however, is that something always comes along to take away the funk. Right now, the antidote just happens to come in the shape of one of the best races of the year – the Irish Champion Stakes.

Some punters shy away from the very top races because

even the tiniest mistake or misjudgement can be disastrous against quality opposition. It's a valid argument but one that, on balance, is far outweighed by the plusses. At the highest level, form is transparent and tends to work out because only genuine horses willing to put it all in get to this class in the first place. Real shocks are almost unheard of. The longest starting price in the Irish Champion Stakes since 1980 was Stanerra's 7–1 in 1983. Plus, there is the considerable consolation that everything is trying for its life. In the Champion Stakes in particular, there is a history of pacemakers ensuring a true end-to-end gallop. Excuses are gratifyingly rare.

From the five-day stage before this Champion Stakes, it is obvious there's going to be a small field that is likely to be dominated by last year's winner, Dylan Thomas, and whatever else Aidan O'Brien decides to throw in. The opening ante-post betting indicates the same. Dylan Thomas is verging on odds-on everywhere. What's interesting, though, as the various firms ring up with the odds, is the wild disparity in the pricing of Finsceal Beo. The double 1,000 Guineas winner hasn't run in almost three months because of all this Bangladeshi ground but the whispers filtering out about her homework are all positive. She has never run beyond a mile but staying ten furlongs has never been considered an issue, and even a first glance at the ten names remaining in the race suggests she is the big danger to the favourite. Everything, though, is in the eye of the beholder.

The Cork firm, Cashmans, is quickest off the mark and makes Finsceal Beo a 5–2 second best. It's when the rest start coming in that any weariness evaporates leaving only a fresh breeze of anticipation. The filly is priced from 11–2 to as high as 8–1.

Rated in front of her are Red Rocks, who won a pretty ordinary Breeders' Cup Turf last year and is a true mile-and-a-half operator. Maraahel who has had more than a dozen attempts at the highest class and failed every time – he ain't going to do it now in a race like this. Then there's Duke Of Marmalade who hasn't won all year and is a definite No. 2 in the Ballydoyle pecking order. All three are rated ahead of Finsceal Beo, which is just plain wrong.

A decisive punter would be on the blower straight away, but ante-post betting has never been my thing. Not for any philosophical reason – just meanness. The idea of lumping on and losing the dough because the horse can't even run is enough to bring me out in hives. So no bets are placed, anywhere.

The following morning, the 8–1 is still available. It's a surprise, but now that the betting is widely available, that's surely not going to last – but it does. The only movement in the betting is all about the favourite dropping to as low as 1–2. That's desperately tight for a horse whose best form is at a mile-and-a-half and must mean he is vulnerable to a horse with a late turn of foot, and the only one with that is Finsceal Beo. Greed overcomes meanness and €100 goes on at 8–1. It's a fantastic bet. By any reckoning, she has one horse to beat and there's a vulnerability to Dylan Thomas at the trip that I like. He's won just once at the top level from four Group 1 starts at ten furlongs this year. Contrast that with a truly outstanding win in the King George, he needs a mile-and-a-half now. This is Eddie G.'s value theory in spades.

At declaration time on Thursday, there are only six remaining in the race and Finsceal Beo is still 8–1 with

William Hill. Her name approximates to 'living legend' in Irish, and that's what that price feels like. Every sinew screams that they've got it wrong.

Now the runners are declared, the price can be taken and its money back if she doesn't run for some reason. Another €100 goes on and €80 more at 7½–1 on Betfair. Later in the day, passing the shop again, curiosity wins out. Sure enough, the 8–1 is still there and another €100 goes on.

All this is on the nose and, even for the each way averse, there is no getting away from the fact that at these prices, it's odds against about Finsceal Beo being in the first two. The automatic reasoning from having boiled the race down to two horses is that this is money from the betting gods. There is no way she is going to be 8–1 on the day. She won't even be 7–1 or 13–2. There's plenty of sevens about now so I put €200 down each way. It's a bet to nothing. The others can't count.

This is now turning into my biggest bet of the year – €780 is already riding on Finsceal Beo. It doesn't take too much rationalising to turn it into €1,000. If this is a serious project, and if this is a serious betting proposition, then it's only nerves at the idea of four digits that are stopping things. €200 has gone down on some hairy bets this year, Power Sharing alone is still chortling his brains out at the idea of any money at all being placed on his resolution. Only a coward would now baulk at getting on the real deal.

The problem is, the closer the race gets, the less adrenalin seems to be pumping. It's always the same; instead of excitement, there's only a slightly nauseous feeling in the pit of my stomach. This really is a lot of money.

One of the perks of my job is a little yellow press badge.

The animal represented on the front of it looks more jennet than racehorse, but it does the job in terms of access to the parade ring. The first of the big-race runners to appear is Finsceal Beo and it's another one of those Lisvale moments. She looks outstanding. The skin on her looks like it's just come out of water. Even though she's completely relaxed about her first race in almost three months, there is a taut power there that puts the lie to any idea the sole filly in the race will be overwhelmed by the maleness around her. Dylan Thomas is a bull of a horse but, physically, Finsceal Beo loses nothing against Red Rocks and the rest.

'Looks well, doesn't she?'

It's always fun when someone whose name you're not sure of starts behaving like you took baths together as kids.

'Hello, umm…'

'Yeah, she's ready, all right.'

He's one of those guys who are at every race meeting and whose only employment seems to be lugging around a pair of enormous binoculars that look like they'd be really useful in the conning tower of a U-boat. It's remarkable how many of this species exist, guys whose faces are as familiar as any jockey's but who don't appear to actually do anything. Maybe they're gentlemen of leisure and independent means, but a lot of them look as if they only get into the track by hanging on to the backs of horseboxes. This guy isn't one of the latter. He's dressed to kill and there are enough badges hanging off his glasses to make him resemble some scalp hunter returning from the prairie. Maybe it's fear of being left alone and being branded some kind of Johnny-No-Mates that's making him talk right now, but he's determined to be friendly.

'I see you went big on Finsceal in the paper this morning.'

'Yeah, I think she's a big price for a horse with only one to beat.'

He throws a look that is probably designed to be shrewd or might just be the result of short-sightedness. 'Kevin rode her in a piece of work on Wednesday. Said she's come on tonnes for the break.' He says quietly out of the side of his mouth, 'She'll win, all right.'

As he says it, someone of far more interest sails into his sights and he's gone. Kevin is Kevin Manning, Finsceal Beo's jockey. It's not beyond the bounds of possibility that this guy might know him – then again, he thinks he knows me.

So often, you believe what you want to believe and this is no exception. Finsceal Beo is the value bet of the year. In the ring, she drops down to 11–2 and 5–1, and that's a good thing. It means I was ahead of the game, everyone else is playing catch up. There's still an each way edge to betting these odds so another €150 each way goes on. After five days of teasing out every possible permutation, I have over €1,000 riding on Finsceal Beo's elegant head.

The gates open and, two minutes later, she passes the post – in last.

Running total: + €4,190

Genius Doesn't Need Money

15 September

A little of the pain inflicted by Finsceal Beo eases a few days later when Ghimaar dots up at Tipperary. The Weld two-year-olds are bombing right now and this latest one is 'expected'. Sure enough, Ghimaar starts favourite and wins easily. Back in third, though, is Majority, the horse I napped in the paper. This tiny ethical dilemma causes no mental anguish whatsoever. In a just and proper world, maybe an SOS should have been beamed to the country to ignore what's been published and go with Ghimaar. However, the assumption that whatever appears in print will be ignored anyway has survived the test of time, so any weeping and gnashing is a result of having only €100 on at 9–4.

It can be a shock to anyone involved in the scribbling game when evidence appears that the stuff is actually being read. This isn't as crazy as it sounds. Normally the rule of thumb is that the only feedback comes from having messed up. This phenomenon ranges from the relatively harmless green-ink scrawl wishing you and yours a slow, screaming death, to the fun of opening up a solicitor's letter. To receive any form of correspondence rooted in normalcy is rare – anything complimentary is rarer still. But sometimes it does happen, and, remarkably, it happens today.

It may be hard to believe but, apparently, there have been occasions during the last few months when my tips in the paper have been hotter than a Bengali navvy's underpants. All this form-study mightn't be generating wads of cash for me but enough of it must be percolating into the scribbling to make it look almost impressive, and at least one man – let's call him Gordon O'Kelly – has been making the most of it.

Gordon is a rare breed of lawyer who writes letters that aren't guaranteed to send one's breakfast hurtling south. He likes a bet – nothing big, mostly accumulators at the weekend, just for an interest – but he bases these on my tips. The idea that such a beast exists is, right now, sending a sizeable proportion of the racing population into paroxysms. The rest are probably wondering if there is a strait-jacket shortage in the Munster region from where said lawyer hales. A consequence of a free democracy is leaving people alone to do the wrong thing if they choose to, but Gordon's judgement in this matter does raise the question of whether or not he should have a driving licence. The only consolation is that, after all this time, he can still afford to indulge in such recklessness and somehow still exhibit an impressive level of class.

When fortune allows him to win, Gordon likes to send a letter containing praise. Sometimes, there's even a gift. On one occasion, there was a hefty restaurant voucher on the back of a fluke that generated enough winnings for a cruise on *QEII*. Accompanying it was the sort of gratitude that owed everything to a generous nature and nothing to the supposed 'skill' that went into a set of tips. But there is no doubt that Gordon is a satisfied customer, something so rare that it brings to mind Basil Fawlty's comment when faced with a similar animal, 'We should have him stuffed!'

In Gordon's latest foray, he has out-done himself. A Galway meeting is the subject of one of his accumulator bets where he selects four horses and jumbles them into a Lucky Fifteen combination. Depending on the prices, even one winner can be enough to cover your costs. In this case, Gordon puts down a €12 Lucky Fifteen which costs him €180. He gets more than that back – a lot more. The combination of Mull On The Run (8–1), Offbeat Fahion (11–4), Via Mantua (5–1) and Frontier Lady (13–2) results in a €37,000-plus beano. Another few thousand comes from a separate Lucky Fifteen where he tragically takes out Frontier Lady and replaces her with Wassily Kandinsky – he is my nap of the day in the paper and, incidentally, the one horse on the whole card that I backed. He gets beaten by a head.

All this I know, because with typical generosity, Gordon chooses to credit his luck to me, but being the big-hearted guy he is, another letter or a phone call isn't enough. Instead, he sends a fax to the Editor's Office, informing Madam that her racing corr' is possessed of 'undoubted genius' and that his salary should be trebled forthwith. OK, the last bit isn't true, but Madam does send a missive of acknowledgement through the chain of command to the Sports Editor who, in turn, informs his underpaid hack that he might not be a complete waste of space after all. There's more extravagant praise in the fax that is too embarrassingly over-the-top for publication but which I still somehow manage to absorb. It's not that hard, there's enough joy crackling off the paper that only a be-knighted jackass could feel anything but happiness for Gordon. However, being happy for Gordon while managing to keep the green-eyed monster away, is proving to be an impossible double to bring up.

If envy really is an ulcer of the soul, then my spirit needs to be hosed down with a few hundred gallons of antacid. It's great for the guy, but it's also horribly unfair. Gordon's doing this for kicks and he secures in a couple of hours what, after six months work, remains maddeningly beyond the horizon for the supposed professional. And he did it on the back of my work! OK, it was hardly work, but still. The amateur is only a few grand short of the target and the pro is staring into a financial Grand Canyon. As Groucho might say, 'This is to natural justice what military music is to music.'

It's taking a considerable effort of will not to spit the dummy. Why isn't this a double celebration? The theory merchants will always insist that combination bets are the preserve of the mug punter, but €40,000 is hard to argue with. Gordy at least has the good grace to say, over the phone, that he will never again darken a bookie's office door. Nobody can be this lucky more than once, he says – no doubt as wads of cash tumble out of his pockets. It doesn't help that he's ringing from the Shelbourne Hotel, one of Dublin's finest. Not surprisingly, he's on one of those weekend breaks that, in time, will become legendary purely because remembering what happened will be impossible. We arrange to finally meet, but somehow miss each other. It's hard to know how, considering one of us is in possession of the biggest grin since Zsa Zsa Gabor first yanked down Porfirio Rubirosa's trousers.

It's at times like these, however, that the real professional will pick up his lip and maintain a true and steady course. Lucky, then, that, in the depths of this despair, an old pal is able to divert my mind elsewhere, at least for a while.

It's St Leger day, both at Doncaster, England, and the Curragh, Ireland. At the Curragh, it's a two-horse race between the O'Brien pair, Yeats and Scorpion. Yeats is a 2–5 favourite, while his next-door neighbour is 4–1. It's lunatic pricing. One has been racing at two-and-a-half miles and the other is a Coronation Cup winner this year. There has always been a question mark about Yeats on fast ground, while Scorpion will run on anything. Only a pound separates them on ratings and yet there is a wild divergence in price. Scorpion's a bet – but he's not *the* bet.

It's hard not to feel some kind of glow about spotting an unraced animal at the start of the season and seeing him turn into a proper racehorse, but that's not the reason for getting stuck into Mahler at Doncaster. The cocky colt, with the inquisitive eye and an ability to transport his greatest fan from deep depression to tearful relief, has a serious chance of winning a classic. There is a ridiculously possessive thing going on, but this is also a coolly logical call. O'Brien is throwing four at the final classic of the English season and Mahler has to have the biggest chance.

Not that the odds reflect this. Instead, it's another Ballydoyle horse, Honolulu, that's a raging hot favourite, the same Honolulu who did for Westlake on that never-to-be-forgotten evening back at Leopardstown. Since then, he has progressed to winning a Listed race at Limerick before running second in the Ebor Handicap at York. The handicap specialists, those boffins who spend their lives pinning figures on flesh and blood, insist a repeat of that run will make him an easy winner. However, this ignores the memory of Limerick where Honolulu's ears revolved like radar once he hit the front. He may not be one to fully trust when it gets tough – and it always gets tough up the half-mile finishing straight at Doncaster.

There are no such doubts about Mahler. After his Derby flop, he went to Royal Ascot and ploughed through muck under Kinane to win the Group 3 Queen's Vase over two miles. That was enough to have him dismissed as a plodder and he did finish only fifth in the Great Voltigeur at York behind today's second-favourite, Lucarno. However, that was on a soft surface too. What this horse needs is fast ground, a fact confirmed by Colm O'Donoghue a week ago.

Colm is one of the better young jockeys in the country and an integral part of the team at Ballydoyle. He rides work there most mornings and is usually called into action if there are more than one or two runners in a major race. That paid off in spades back in May when he won the French Guineas on Astronomer Royal. Not surprisingly, on the back of a classic win, he's riding better than ever, and it's not hard to be happy for him since Colm is a naturally amiable guy. Subjected to a chat between races at Leopardstown, he gracefully pretended to ponder my opinion on the Leger.

'Mahler can't have the ground fast enough,' he says. 'He likes it like a road, and he'll keep going. He's got some stride – just keeps lengthening.'

'You might even get to ride him yourself?'

'I don't know. It wouldn't be the worst thing in the world, I suppose.'

Ultimately, Colm ends up on Acapulco and, once again, it's Kinane on board Mahler. That's hardly a negative. Aged forty-eight, there is a depressing inevitability about the whispers that suggest the great jockey is past his best but, on any big day, there's no one else you'd want. The biggest races demand cold calculation and no one has ever looked at that famously determined face and reckoned his brain is doing anything else but whirring furiously. It looks good. The ground is right and O'Brien's pre-race quotes are encouraging. Lucarno is the one to beat, but he's not sure to get the mile-and-three-quarters. Great horses have been beaten in the Leger – the likes of Shergar and Alleged – because class gets you to the two-furlong pole and, after that, it's all about slogging stamina. That's where Mahler will win it.

Of course, there would be even more confidence behind such a statement if a certain Finsceal Beo hadn't run like a hound last week. Nothing has come to light to explain how a double classic winner can run like that. Her trainer is quoted as saying that he can find nothing wrong with her. It ends up being filed under 'one of those days'. It certainly was. Only a loon would ignore such an experience and light-heartedly pile in again but, in a way, Gordy's good fortune helps a little. OK, he won a lot of money but his initial stake was €180. It came off this week, but how many days have gone by when it hasn't? It adds up quickly when you're losing. So, nothing ventured, nothing gained…

Mahler's a 7–1 shot in the ante-post betting, so it's the same deal as last week. From declaration time on Thursday, it's non-runner and money back, so the Ghimaar profit is played up. On the exchanges, Mahler is much the same and another hundred goes on. It feels like the race will never come after that. How people get stuck into big races months in advance is a mystery. Waiting for the outcome is like waiting for exam results – there's the same conflict between wanting to get it over with and fear of the possible outcome. On the morning of the race, Mahler starts drifting out to nearly 11–1 on the exchanges as Honolulu gets hit harder than Pearl Harbor. But then Mahler starts to come back in with a vengeance. It's enough to dismiss any suspicion that he's not fancied. Another €200 goes on at sevens and is joined by a similar sum on Scorpion at 4–1. To tie the bundle up nicely, there's a €100 double the pair of them. It comes to an almost €8,500 pay-off.

The double-up is probably Gordon's influence. It isn't a smart bet because, if Mahler does win, €800 will go on to Scorpion and, although he has a good chance, he doesn't really have the kind of chance that would justify that stake. Still, he has only one horse to beat – just like Finsceal Beo.

Any sickly feeling that the mention of Finsceal Beo name brings about vanishes when the gates open at Doncaster. Kinane immediately sends Mahler to the front and the pair dominate from the start. It's lovely to watch; there's an exuberance in that scything stride that leaves no doubt – Mahler is having fun. Ears pricked, and with an occasional glance sideways at the camera vehicle travelling alongside, he gallops powerfully across the newly laid turf with a brio that only athletes at the peak of their physical prowess might fully understand. Up top, Kinane peeps around a few times just to keep tabs on who's queuing up behind. There's nothing on his tail to worry about. The dangers are all loitering at the back, eager to conserve energy off the good pace.

It's going like clockwork. Races occasionally pan out like this, as if there's a remorseless logic to what's happening. Mind you, it's rare, and even rarer in the very best races. Kinane was there too when Galileo won the Derby in 2001. A Guineas winner was stuck to his tail but never once did Galileo look like anything but the dominant horse. Mahler is not as good as his dad but Kinane takes another peek at halfway and decides to pick things up. A couple of lengths quickly open. It's not silky-smooth, but that's not what the Leger demands. Turning in, and facing up the long straight, Kinane starts to lower himself into Mahler and slowly but surely crank up the pressure.

Most of those behind are in trouble already. A quick scan of the field reveals most of the jockeys rowing furiously. Mahler's got them all at it, except for one. Lucarno is still going easily; Honolulu is tracking him but Murtagh is hard at work. Lucarno is the danger. He finished fourth in the Derby, well ahead of Mahler, but as they pass the two-furlong marker, he's into virgin territory.

Kinane hasn't fully gone for the whip yet. That's a great

sign. With the top guys, reaching for the stick is usually the last desperate throw of the dice. That's not to say that every sinew in that wiry frame isn't straining, hands changing on the reins in the unmistakable signal to Mahler that he should go even faster. The horse responds with the sort of grit that has me staring pop-eyed at the screen.

Lucarno's class provokes a surge that takes him clear of the rest but which comes at the cost of a drift left closer to the leader. This is going to be an eyeball-to-eyeball slog that, surely, Mahler is better equipped for. Kinane seems to sense it too and, if anything, he looks to get even lower in the saddle. And then, everything changes.

As Lucarno looms alongside, Mahler takes a funny step. It would be nice to be able to say something more technical, like he changed leads, but it's too exaggerated for that. This is a bunny hop executed by the biggest rabbit you've ever seen. Dayjur famously threw away a Breeders' Cup win when he jumped a shadow at Belmont Park but there's no shadow here. There's no reason for it at all. Mahler suddenly decides to take a running jump through my heart. His impetus is fatally interrupted and Lucarno gets a couple of lengths ahead. Inside the final furlong, Mahler comes back at him but, at the line, he's still a length short.

Kinane says the jump might have cost him the win which hardly helps morale. It is obvious there would have been a photo-finish, and who knows what Lucarno had left to repel a true stayer. He was impressive at the end but he wasn't fully pressed. The hair-tearing frustration of it all comes from the suspicion of a vulnerability that hasn't been fully exploited.

Things don't improve ten minutes later.

It's money back if Scorpion wins. For most of the trip, he leads and looks good but, right at the end, he gets touched off by Yeats. This time there's only half-a-length in it, but it might as well be half a world away.

Maybe there's a spare zero there.

Running total: + €3,565

The St Bernard Casino

1 October

It takes a couple of weeks before even the idea of betting doesn't cause a rash, but the greatest gambling spree in the entire horse business begins the rehabilitation process. If there's one thing a yearling sale can do, it is to allow even the most spendthrift punter to seem sober.

The Goff's sales complex in Kill is no Caesar's Palace. It's a large lump of concrete sticking out of a flat field next to the Dublin motorway. Lines of cold, grey stables extend outwards, like the tentacles of a cash-hungry octopus. When it's not in business, the whole thing could be a Stalag. When it's in business, even the gaudiest Vegas casino can't compete.

If racecourses are gaming tables, then these sales are where you get your chips. The more money you shove through the slot, the brighter and more expensive the chips are. Except, here, it's possible to choose your own, which gives you a slight edge when it comes to beating the odds, but not so much that buying a yearling still isn't a colossal leap of faith.

A total of 600 of these pubescent bluebloods are scheduled to parade around the ring over the next three days in Ireland's most valuable auction of the year. Over €60 million will be spent. That's an average of €100,000 for each animal, and maybe one in five will end up winning a race – and not even a good race, just a race. The majority probably won't even make it to a racecourse. Right now, there's no knowing which of them will turn out to be useless and which one might just turn out to be an embryonic champion that wins the Derby and ends up breeding a dynasty. That's both the incentive and the problem.

None of them has even had a saddle put on them yet. All anyone can go on is the way they walk and behave themselves as they skitter around outside before entering the ring. It's like taking a batch of primary school kids and trying to decide which of them is going to be a great footballer. They might look the part, and Daddy might have been Pele, but never forget that none of Pele's kids could play worth a damn.

Statistically, the process is enough to make the roulette wheel in Circus Circus look like a sound business proposition, and yet buyers come here from around the globe in a stubborn wildebeestian trek, ignoring any snapping jaws of penury and, instead, concentrating on that next spindly legged adolescent racehorse who might, just might, be the real deal. Next to this, Vegas is for virgins.

It's an intoxicating mixture of childish dreams and wolfish greed, laced with any amount of deceit, naïvety, snobbishness and bullshit you care to add. The beautiful animals nervously pace around for two to three minutes while spotters' yelps interrupt the auctioneer's 'be-da-da-be-be-da-da-be' drone and the red lights that translate all those euro into dollars, pounds and yen shine out neutrally, indifferent to the total. If there is any demand for a horse at all, then bids increase in tens of thousands. The real top ones go up in steps of fifty thousand. If there are more than two bidders, and the spotters are shouting over themselves, the red lights can struggle to keep up. After a while, the blur of garish technology and rampant spending means it takes at least €500,000 to shake away numbing indifference to what is high-finance's equivalent to Gordy's Lucky Fifteen. Except, here, the figures seem to have only a fleeting relevance to the world as most of us know it.

Just outside the auditorium, a chance meeting with David Wachman promises the inside-track on which of the 200 horses for sale today might make the big money.

'Let's see,' he says, skimming through the thick catalogue, and then muttering an oath. 'This one will make a few quid,' he says before strolling inside where Lot 59 has just entered.

A Dansili filly, who looks nice and shiny and in no obvious way different from the animal before her that made €65,000, reaches €230,000. The hammer comes down and a helpful 'Thank you, David Wachman' from the auctioneer is the only indication that the buyer was almost prevented from spending €¼ million by my fuzzy-headed request to have my card marked. It's enough to cause a flush of embarrassment as

Wachman hurriedly walks past again, eager to find the next expensive would-be champion.

It's not as if there aren't enough characters around here with a lot more time on their hands and a lifetime's experience of appearing to know exactly where a card should be marked.

Just as at the racetrack, looking to be 'in the know' is of primary importance to a lot of people. Except here, the process usually involves plummier accents, deeper tans and an almost religious devotion to Burberry. It's all part of the sales uniform. Chancers struggling to raise the cost of dinner try to look as if they're on the verge of splashing out €1 million on a Sadlers Wells, often while wearing the sort of flat cap that's wide enough to make the owner look like he is transporting a tweed frying pan on his head.

To us rubber-neckers peering into the process, it all seems alien, some weird parallel universe where corduroy is fashionable. It's certainly very easy to dismiss it as one long penis-flexing exercise for the too rich and the too bored. Over the years, as racing's two superpowers – Coolmore and Godolphin – have faced each other across sales rings around the world, there has always been the temptation to dismiss the process as one that could be resolved much more cheaply if Sheikh Mohammed and John Magnier just went into the nearest gents and had a peep. But that's too simplistic.

Statistically, it might look like an elaborate way to flush a lot of money down the toilet but each year, from Kentucky to Deauville, to Kill and then on to Newmarket, the travelling circus keeps rolling, and keeps churning the sort of cash that would maintain a small nation going for quite some time. Somehow, it all works because the dream of owning a champion is so intoxicating. If it wasn't, no one would be shivering here on a cold October day – and no one knows how to work it better than the man who suddenly now decides to stand only a couple of feet away.

As with most powerful men, John Magnier is rarely alone. Maybe when he tends to his ablutions, he might experience solitude, but, then again, there might be someone tailing him in there too. Even if there isn't, a lot of people still want to believe there might be. The myth has become almost as powerful as the man because, when it comes to this game, J.M. really is the horse-player's wet dream, not just in Ireland, but around the world. He's also a business talent of such steely focus that it is said that the softest part of him is his teeth. When Alex Ferguson decided some years ago to get all-Govan about Rock Of Gibralter, the racehorse that he and Magnier famously shared during his racing career, there was no one in racing who, for one moment, believed he was going to get any joy. Throwing shapes at someone whose poster is probably above the bed of every billionaire businessman between Tipperary and Taipei was a painful lesson in who's in the real premiership.

Despite the exposure that little spat generated, Magnier remains an enigmatic figure. Compared to some of his business and sporting contemporaries, he presents a sphinx-like inscrutability to the world. Apparently, this is deliberate, because of Magnier's reported view that personal publicity is cheap. Some who know him put his unease down to shyness, although that hardly squares with a professional reputation that suggests he is about as shy as a toilet seat.

Just as standing next to Weld at Galway resulted in a

heightened degree of self-consciousness, the same thing happens here as, inches away, the Coolmore posse huddle into a mumbling conference that might result in a multimillion-euro investment – or a decision about what to eat for lunch. Even from this close distance, it's impossible to know. It's like something from a Le Carré novel, all nods and significant glances, a mysterious patois that can make or break in a matter of minutes. In the middle of it all, Magnier himself peers panoramically across an environment that, by now, must be as familiar to him as backstage is to Keith Richards. It ain't home but it feels like it, a place in which to be comfortable, a bit like his footwear.

The man who's richer than Croesus is wearing sneakers that, at first glance, look like they come from the house of St Bernard. After hours of cords and waxed jackets, it comes as a shock to find that the most important figure here is padding about in Dunnes Stores' finest. Everything else is just as you'd expect: the striped shirt with the white collar has a silk cravat stuffed inside and the Barbadian tan is topped off by a rakishly tilted cowboy hat. But he's supermarket shod. There are plenty who rate footwear as a pretty effective indicator of the person. Magnier's father-in-law, Vincent O'Brien, for instance, is apparently a stickler for a well-polished brogue. On this evidence, he must keep his eyes well above the equator when the family gets together.

However, for those of us with our financial arses considerably closer to the ground, there is something undeniably cool about a billionaire traipsing about in the same gear as the guy who mooches around the ring shovelling up expensively bred horse manure. The old line about money not talking so much as shouting is only true up to a point. In fact real money only needs to whisper and if J.M. chooses to walk on the cheap, it's a good bet that there'll be some shell suits parading around Goff's next year.

Daydreams of a lot of double-barrelled wannabes walking around in hoodies and sweatpants quickly disappear as the next-door huddle breaks and Magnier's crew assume a pose of disinterest. It fools no one. The horse in the ring is by Sadlers Wells, the veteran Coolmore stallion whose potency has netted his owner a fortune over the last twenty years. It's obvious 'the boys' want him and every eye in the place swivels to the one place as the bidding begins.

It's remarkable how difficult it is to stay motionless. To stay absolutely still for even thirty seconds takes a real effort: something will inevitably start itching, there will always be an insect that views your eye as an aircraft carrier, or a rogue virus that has been dormant for weeks will suddenly pick its moment to explode into sneezing fury. And, as moments go, there's nothing quite like being faced by shark-eyed auctioneers who are in charge of spotters with better vision than your average sniper. An urgent meeting with the bank manager is only one wrong blink away.

Just a step in front of me is Demi O'Byrne, the man who does the actual bidding for Coolmore. Magnier stands next to him as O'Byrne sends the red lights flashing quickly past the €250,000 mark. It's no wonder that spotters require good eyesight. O'Byrne's gesture to signify a bid is a tiny almost irritable swat of his catalogue. To the untrained eye, it's nothing. After just two minutes in Goff's, it results in a €300,000 purchase. When the hammer comes down, Magnier resumes his place in the eye of the huddle and the monosyllabic muttering starts all over again.

The anaesthetising effect of so much invisible money means that daydreams are inevitable. It's impossible to mosey outside amongst the wax jackets and not wonder what they see that makes one yearling more valuable than another. Those pedigrees on the page count for a lot but no one ever sent a pedigree up the gallops. The usual cant about a nice, fluid walk, as well as a good eye, doesn't cut it either. Every one of the 600 lots are here precisely because they can put one foot in front of the other and aren't visually impaired. Maybe the Burberrys swarming around the stables, intently peering at the horses being walked up and down in front of them, simply aren't able to articulate what cuts the ice here, although the same Burb's have the linguistic skill to make spending thousands on a glorified pony sound like the business opportunity of a lifetime.

Instead, the reality is that everything is in the eye of the beholder. One person's must-have is another's discard. As one trainer remarks: it's like going to a club and fancying a woman walking past, 'You just have to tailor your tastes to your budget!'

Much of this tailoring takes place around the roofed parade ring that circles the chute down which the horses go to be sold. After days of being hauled out of their box to be poked, prodded and primped, the yearlings then have about half an hour of mooching around before their date with destiny. Final decisions are made here. Is that bay with the straight shoulder worth going over €100,000 for? How far will that pedigree take him when the owner wants a miler? Is that Exceed And Excel really a stallion to rely on? And why's that journo twat taking up so much space?

The daydream has gone into overdrive over Lot 149. This is a tall, rangy bay colt by Nayef who's plodding around the ring as if bored by the whole exercise. A few others are squealing and skittering about, nerves getting the better of them, but 149 looks nothing but disdainful. If the stuff about walking well means anything, then this fella has got to be the business. There's a fluidity and an ease to his movement that looks great. He's also a tall horse with a nice depth of shoulder. Unlike anything else here, there's a bump in his forehead that he seems to have inherited from his dad, a sort of misplaced Roman nose that doesn't help him in the prettiness stakes but does lend a certain patrician quality. That's what his name should be, Patrician – with any luck the moniker hasn't been taken already.

It's a little embarrassing to be daydreaming so childishly, but there's comfort to be had that it isn't the only juvenile behaviour going on around here. Even for sellers, whose business depends on the best possible price, there is always the dream that this latest yearling could be the champion to define a lifetime. It's what the whole crazy circus is all about. Some people are just able to hide their hope better than others.

People like Barry Hills. The English trainer signals for 149 to leave the ring and stand next to him. Hills briefly looks in the direction of the horse's genitals and appears satisfied that everything is where it ought to be. Then he stands back, then in again at 149's shoulder. The proximity of the stranger makes the horse step away slightly but only in the way that anyone would if an unfamiliar little man in a silly hat started invading your personal space. Hills doesn't give much away, just stands back again and purses his lips slightly. It's a good sign when such a high-profile trainer takes an interest and, sure enough, twenty minutes later, the Nayef that should be called Patrician emerges from the auditorium having made €110,000.

That's all very well, but since he isn't likely to see a race-course for at least a year, it produces the kind of gratification that maybe only Mr and Mrs Sting with their penchant for lengthy tantric nookie might enjoy. For those of us with constitutions more suitable for sprinting than distance running, a more immediate release is needed. Just as well, then, that Provincial's coming up at the meeting in Roscommon.

On the face of it, Provincial is not the brightest bet in the world. He's having the first race of his career in a big field of juvenile maidens. There's also the lingering suspicion that if Provincial really is as good as he's supposed to be, then why's he running at a country course rather than the likes of the Curragh or Leopardstown? Other gossip suggests that Kevin Prendergast's Sufad will beat him anyway. But he's still the one to risk a tiptoe back into the water. Dermot Weld has said he has a very good crop of two-year-olds and the word for weeks now has been that this Khalid Abdullah-owned colt is right up there with the best of them.

Soon after the race starts, Provincial is at the back of the field and doesn't look at all happy taking the first tight bend that brings them towards the straight. He doesn't appear entirely comfortable taking the turn in either and, as Pat

Smullen steers him to the outside, there's at least ten lengths to make up. Provincial's head comes up at the pressure that Smullen is forced to exert but he doesn't chuck it in. He's desperately green, but game enough to keep pulling out more. Sufad does turn out to be the danger and the pair of them lock horns for the final furlong. Sufad briefly looks like fighting back but, at the line, Provincial is just in front.

€100 at 7–4 is hardly going to make a dent in the overall picture but there's no getting away from the rush that the close finish provides, especially when, for once, it goes the right way. And, thankfully, it'll help pay for a few more chips to throw on the table.

Running total: + €3,740

Billy Hogarth's Slow Progress

12 October

The €45,000 barrier has been passed. In fact, the total sum is more like €47,000. So, it's a case of job done, and thank you very much indeed. At least that's what Gordy says – 'Thank you very much, indeed.' Then he apologises for having said that a betting shop would never see him again, but he was killing a few minutes outside court and what better way to kill time than to nip into a bookies and jot down a €4 Lucky Fifteen that pays off almost €5,500. As Gordy was collecting, other punters were touching him, as if rubbing some expensively tailored relic.

His bet comes up at a Friday Dundalk meeting. They're racing at night there now, a new floodlit experience that seems to be catching on in a big way. There are traditionalists who sniff that camels could be racing outside and none of the clientele inside the restaurants and bars would care less, but that's what the powers that be at Dundalk appear to want: a migratory younger crowd that view the track as a viable way of socialising and don't care very much what species is providing the entertainment. Greyhound racing has perfected the system; now it's the gee-gees' turn.

The upside is that for every 100 booze-hounds, there might just be one who bothers to pay attention and ends up feeling that emotional pull towards what remains for a lot of us the sexiest damned sport in the world. Football might be the most democratic, but the beautiful game often turns into an exercise in holding your nose while the latest over-hyped, one-season wonder flexes his social skills. In Ireland, hurling and Gaelic football dominate the summer and are as much blighted as defined by parish-pump rivalries which are the result of a scrape of a civil service pencil on a map centuries ago in London. Rugby here still retains an unattractive class element and golf isn't so much a sport as an exercise in wearing polo shirts.

Racing, on the other hand, contains enough backstabbing intrigue and roistering deceit to make even the raunchiest soap opera look like a school nativity play. At the top end, there's more money than anyone knows what to do with and irrespective of finance, everyone gets to play in a boisterously earthy environment that seems to have a peculiarly altitude-depressing impact on the hydraulics of many people's underwear. It's a daily drama that manages to create a niche for almost everyone, prince or punter. In a golf club, wearing the wrong shoes gets you thrown out.

Sometimes, however, being on the verges of the drama is preferable to being slap bang in the middle. Kieren Fallon wins the Prix de l'Arc de Triomphe on Dylan Thomas and, the following morning, turns up at the Old Bailey for the start proper of his race-fixing trial. Five others are accused too, but the focus remains on one man. Before the Arc, Fallon admitted his confidence has been shaken by the whole process. He's not wrong. This summer, his riding has been terrible a lot of the time. There have probably been more howlers in the last four months than in his whole career. In particular, an inept effort on Listen in a Group 2 at the Curragh in August had all the signs of a jockey whose nerves were shot to hell. And yet, he comes up with the goods when it matters most in the Arc. Even those who can't stand the man have to admit it's a crying shame seeing such a talent scurrying into a court house.

Even a Fallon at full power, however, can't turn William Hogarth into what a lot of people hoped he might be. Way back in the spring at that Ballydoyle open day, the High Chaparral colt out of Mountain Holly was the first two-year-old nominated by Aidan O'Brien as being in the smart class. When you consider that horses like the Guineas winner King Of Kings have filled a similar position in the past, it's hardly surprising that more than a few of us filed that breeding away at the back of our minds and waited for a name. The original William Hogarth was fond of a joke but there's nothing particularly funny about this punchline.

Before his debut at the Curragh, there were reports of ante-post bets for the following year's Derby, the sort of stuff that, nine times out of ten, provides bookmakers with the chance for more newspaper exposure and little else. It's hard to completely ignore, though, so it comes as something of a let-down when Billy eventually does run and he's only the third string of the three O'Brien runners. In itself, that isn't an automatic dream-destroyer. Famously, Footstepsinthesand was another newcomer ridden by Colm O'Donogue who was initially dismissed as a 10–1 shot on his debut only to trot up the following year and win the 2,000 Guineas. But Billy doesn't appear overly keen about making much of an impression on the sands of time. He finishes sixth in a first start that is encouraging enough on its own terms but leaves any ideas of a classic looking faintly ridiculous. Still, a lot of great horses have been beaten on their first ever starts – think of Sir Ivor, High Chaparral, even Authorized.

Hogarth's next chance to prove himself is a mile maiden at Gowran which could be a very different matter, especially since Fallon is here and not in a court room. Billy opens a 7–4 shot but drifts. That's not a huge concern; it happens a lot as bookmakers try to find out the lie of the land. The horse looks well, alert and with a distinctive white blaze that is immediately sent into the lead once the gates open. This is good, and also very bad.

Seamus Heffernan has won a lot of races this year riding these Ballydoyle two-year-olds from the front. From a punting point of view, it's a reassuringly straightforward way of going about business but it's not really Fallon's style. His habit is more often to try and educate by bringing them through horses. That can cause heart attacks in those of us with quite a lot of money at stake but O'Brien himself appreciates it. He can afford to think long term, while those of us with €500 to €200 about Billy suspect immediately that Fallon riding this way means this is a hit-and-hope job: he's using that experience from a month ago and hoping to get the others at it quickly. A real potential top-notcher wouldn't be ridden like this and so it proves. Early in the straight, Billy is challenged and quickly passed. He fades to a well-beaten fourth. The only consolation from tearing up the ticket is that it isn't an ante-post voucher on the Derby.

There's better luck a couple of hours later when Worldy Wise wins a handicap in good style, defying ten stone and €500 to €100 on his back. But it isn't long before reminders come of the danger of placing too much faith in the Ballydoyle juvenile team. It's been quite a wait since Derby weekend but Alessandro Volta, the well-backed O'Brien horse in that maiden won by Lisvale, finally gets a second start in a Wednesday meeting at Navan. The son of Montjeu looks as imperious as ever, and also impressively calm. It's typical of the sire to mix mental brittleness with brilliance but the vibes on track are positive enough to suggest a visit to a shrink isn't on the cards for his son just yet.

It's turning into a funny October. Normally at this time of year, everyone's eyes are glued for horses going off the boil after a long season. Previously shiny coats start to get hairy and clip lines start to appear. But instead there's an Indian summer going on. The ground at Navan is good to firm whereas usually at this meeting, everyone's ankle deep in muck. Maybe muck would have suited Alessandro better because, after looking like launching a winning challenge at the two furlong pole, he fizzles out to third behind a 10–1 shot called Moiqen.

The rest of the Worldy Wise profit, and a little more too, disappears a couple of days later in a Listed race at Dundalk. It's the Star Appeal Stakes, named after the most famous horse to win at the track, the subsequent 1975 Prix de l'Arc de Triomphe winner. There's another Paris link in the race as Minneapolis ran in a Group 1 at Longchamp just twelve days ago. Not surprisingly, he was well beaten there but, even less surprising, is the fact that he's back here. That trip to France came after a win on the all-weather just days before which oozed class. Minneapolis looked a different animal on the synthetic surface. Tonight's the same course and distance and, although a much tougher race, there's no dismissing the memory of how good he looked before.

Minneapolis is second-favourite behind a maiden called Great War Eagle who was an obviously unlucky loser in his only race at the Curragh. Betting on 'shoulda' winners is a dangerous exercise, however. Horses that find trouble in a race once often tend to do the same again. Great War Eagle doesn't look like one of those who find trouble through a basic lack of pace, but how he's favourite is a mystery. Minneapolis, on the other hand, is a perfect opportunity to test the theory that course form on the polytrack is a huge advantage.

There's almost 5–1 available on the exchanges which, combined with a 7–2 starting price, means a pay-off of over €1,100.

It looks OK at the start when Heffernan misses the break and quickly tacks across to the rail. Ballydoyle's number two jockey has been wonderfully consistent all year and, once again, he secures a good run around to the straight where Minneapolis picked up so well for him a fortnight earlier.

Except, this time, he doesn't. Instead, it's Great War Eagle who gets up in a photo.

Ben Franklin's belief was that energy and persistence conquers everything, which only shows that being brilliantly bright and variously talented is no barrier to sometimes spouting rubbish. Prolonged exposure to the morale-sapping reality of losing on the horses is a harsh antidote to any ideas of certitude. In fact, it's maybe just as well the season is winding down because it is turning into a long lesson in humility.

Compared to the still-sleekly coated creatures out on the track, some of us are showing the all too familiar signs of a long year. Any dazzle from the floodlights is immediately lost in simple dull-eyed determination to make it through to the end of another meeting. There are just over three weeks to the end: only twenty-three days until the fateful tot up; 550 hours to the final black and white bottom line; 33,000 minutes until... well you get the idea – except it won't be the end as we used to know it.

The face of racing in Ireland is actually changing forever because of Dundalk. This all-weather stuff will keep going until December, and will kick off again in February. It's new ground for the game and, commercially, it never made sense to race for just seven months of the year and then shut down completely. In that sense, Ireland is only catching up with the rest of the world. Things are never going to be quite the same again.

Running total: + €3,440

Everyone's Favourite
Day-Release Programme

22 October

It was a gloriously sunny day when the season kicked off back in March, but now that the Curragh is hosting its last meeting of the year, things are more normal. Cold rain tears across the famous plain as if late for a hot date. Heavy mist disguises the Wicklow Mountains to the east, and only a church steeple manages to peep through the murk in nearby Kildare town. The deserted stands echo to occasional bursts of laughter around their cavernous emptiness. Apart from grey concrete and green grass, the only flashes of colour come from tarpaulined juggernauts flashing past on the motorway half-a-mile away. A shale, black infield where marquees were put up for the midsummer classics is now deserted, pallets and blocks leaning against a timber fence that creaks and bulges against the wind. On a cold, wet Monday, the creaking is just about the only atmosphere in the place.

There might be 1,000 bodies in here, including those jockeys going out for the first race. They look like a platoon of mini-Captain Oates figures who've just told their pals in the weigh room that they may be some time. When they mount up, there are no more than ten people watching them around the parade ring. It's hard not to think the spectators are on some kind of day-release programme, where the freedom to roam outweighs the fear of pneumonia. But at least they haven't had to pay in. It's a free admission day, which is flagged as a marketing ploy but feels like an acknowledgement to the fact that no one's coming anyway – so why pay someone to man the gates? If money does set the world in motion then, right now, it feels like we're standing still. Maybe that's because the real money isn't here.

Age Of Chivalry is a heavily backed favourite for the first and wins easily, costing the on-course bookmakers most of the €29,000 generated on the race. On Betfair alone, turnover was well over the €500,000 mark. It's impossible to accurately calculate how much the race generated in betting shops and on off-shore telephone accounts, but the safest bet of the day is that the figure comes to a hell of a lot more than €29,000. Down at the ring, Eddie G. stares mournfully across an almost deserted betting ring and mutters about there being way too much racing, 'We're diluting the whole product.'

It's a typical scene at many midweek meetings. Getting people through the gates doesn't matter nearly as much as it used to because racetracks are getting substantial income from the television pictures being beamed into betting shops and homes. Only habit keeps many of us returning to bookmakers for our betting fix. In twenty years time, the idea of going to the races and handing over folding money to a large man standing on a box will probably seem as redundant as chalk and a board. It's already happening, even Down Under.

The simplicity of the gambling system in Australia makes the complex web of bookmaker chains, television rights, betting tax and government handouts on this side of the globe seem even more hopelessly convoluted. On-course bookmakers compete with an on-course Tote just as here but, off-course, the betting shops aren't privately owned and profits are ploughed back, in a self-perpetuating loop that enables the whole sport to thrive. But even there, concerns are growing at the impact of internet and off-shore telephone betting. Bookmakers at the likes of Flemington and Moonee Valley are feeling the pinch. Percentage turnover is going down, and this is in a country where the inhabitants are not renowned for being shy when it comes to having a bet.

In the United States, racing only survives in some states because of on-site casinos. Mindless coin pumping might not seem the most exciting way to spend an afternoon but it sure seems to be profitable. So much so that a lot of meetings in the US take place in front of tiny crowds outside while, inside, the slots rattle and hum until they're hot. Such a nightmare scenario isn't around the corner here just yet. In fact, the growth of the major festivals continues to increase overall attendance figures, but on a bread-and-butter day, when the real money is being generated on the pictures, and with only a handful of people on the ground, it feels ominous. In fact, it mightn't be too long before this wet Monday morgue will seem riotous in comparison to what goes on.

What will never change, however, is that the real specialists will always be standing at the rails, because that's where the horses are. And where there are horses, there is gossip – the sort of gossip that can sweep up even the most hardened sceptic and take him along on one of those this-can't-lose rides. When it comes off, there is no more exhilarating sensation. When it doesn't, even the one man and his dog on duty can make the world seem too crowded.

Maybe that's why there's something mildly therapeutic about this isolation because, twenty-four hours ago, it felt like everyone was bouncing around like pebbles in a flood.

It hadn't felt like a day to bet, which is why no real money changed hands, just the dangerously metaphysical version that substitutes for the real thing when you bet over the phone. Sufad, the two-year-old that pressed Provincial all the way to the line at Roscommon, is having his second start in an auction maiden. These are races confined to the offspring of sires who are not in the stratospheric price range of the real top-notch stallions. There are some real crows mooching around the parade ring with number-cloths on their backs. A colt of the Aga Khan's called Kargan rears up and tries to kick the lad leading him round. When someone else takes over the rein, he has a pop at him, too. Kargan is the second-favourite. There are twenty-eight of them in total over seven furlongs, but if Kargan's second in the betting, then Sufad really is the heavy odds-on favourite that a cursory look at the field in the morning indicated he would be.

I had barely taken a couple of steps into the track before I heared that Sufad is fancied out of sight by Kevin Prendergast and that he's passed the post already. The shock comes from seeing him open at 6–4. It's one of those rub-your-eyes moments: 4–6 maybe, but this has to be a mistake. Sufad, however, lengthens to 2–1, tightens to 15–8 a couple of times, but keeps returning to twos. In the ring, Virgil is prowling around like a cheetah trying to assess which helpless calf will make the best eating. It all adds up. There are only a couple of minutes to get on but, in the modern betting world, a bet is always just a couple of digits away – €800 to €400 is secured just as the field jump off.

It never feels right. Sufad travels well enough to halfway but McDonogh doesn't have the taut grip of the reins that you like to see in a supposed good-thing. He starts to niggle at the three pole and, a furlong later, ends up throwing everything at his horse. Even at this stage of the season, nothing can stop that empty-stomach sensation of watching another major bet start to struggle. In fairness to Sufad, he doesn't engage reverse gear, just keeps going at the one pace, as the 10–1 shot Yali pounces late to win. The favourite is back in fourth.

It really should be easier to cope with reverses by now, and it is, to an extent – the extent being that the Leonard Cohen slow march of old has disappeared. Now, it's more of a Nick Cave tiptoe through the puddles. People are no longer approaching me and asking if there's been a death in the family. There's even enough resilience to come to the Curragh today and stand out in the rain to watch the runners in the parade ring before another seven-furlong, two-year-old maiden. This is a straightforward one, with no breeding restrictions, which is just as well because Arizona John has the sort of pedigree that guarantees interest. His father, Rahy, is a Kentucky stallion with a $60,000 stud fee and his mother, Preseli, won the Group 1 Moyglare Stud Stakes in 1999. His family connections are eye-catching and there was enough in Arizona John's debut at Gowran to encourage belief he will be a different customer now.

The favourite is a Ballydoyle newcomer, Washington Irving, who just happens to have an entry for a Group 1 race in five days' time. A furtive chat in the weigh room reveals that he's good, maybe not absolute top-rate, classic-winning good, but certainly talented enough to win a back-end maiden first time of asking. The encouragement comes from all the evidence this year that going in first time up is a big ask. Arizona John was desperately green on his own debut but even in the parade ring, he looks a different customer – tighter, and a little more knowing. Kinane is here to ride, which is no mean signal since he was riding in Toronto last night, and he and John Oxx have already scored with Age Of Chivalry.

Arizona John does indeed behave like a different animal. That wide-eyed disbelief at what was asked of him at Gowran has been replaced by an impressive professionalism. Kinane puts him straight into the lead and the colt is gun-barrel straight up the middle of the Curragh. The seventeen other runners queue up behind but every single one of them is being pushed at the two-furlong pole and Kinane still hasn't moved.

If life really is a series of disappointments, with one real big one at the end, then this is miniature rehearsal for the final doozie. Appearances can always be deceptive and, in this case, Kinane is hanging on to nothing. Arizona John is giving everything he has already so when his jockey gets busy, there isn't a whole pile left to pull out. Like Sufad, it's not a question of bottling a tough situation: he's game enough, just not good enough. Washington Irving is behind him but two others are in front.

Another €400 at 3–1 disappears. Virgil's system of betting each way at those odds would have meant at least something back but it's too late now to be exercising prudence. It's becoming increasingly obvious that what's needed is a late-late spectacular.

Running total: + €2,640

It's Fate – With a Plan

29 October

It's a funny thing, putting everything in the hands of fate. There's a certain shame – but also a wonderful reassurance. After all, passing the buck to whomever or whatever may be twiddling the knobs lets you off the hook.

Call it fate, destiny or plain juju, but there are some racing days when everything clicks and many others that fall apart. For the lack of any better way of describing the sensation, let's say it's a question of whether your eye is in or out. Calculating a race depends on a lot of variables and everyone brings their own prejudices and opinions to the task. If your eye is in, however, it's remarkable how the criteria brought to one race can apply to the others. That's how streaks start.

This Bank Holiday Monday begins with a speculative €50 double. My first hunch, Plan, is predicted to start a 5–2 favourite for the seven-furlong maiden, which is pretty good for a Ballydoyle two-year-old, and Princess Rose Anne has the sort of profile that sticks out in the Nursery. Jim Bolger's runner has had four runs, the last of them over five furlongs. Now that she's back up to seven, and with a good draw, Princess Rose Anne's worth a shot.

It doesn't feel like the usual end-of-season run in at Leopardstown. Normally this meeting, and the final one of the season, take place on desperate ground, in desperate weather and, often, with desperate results. But, this time, the going is actually on the fast side and there's enough warmth in the sun to put a bounce into even the most jaded step.

The betting in the opening two-year-old fillies' maiden is wide open. Those that have run don't look much and clearly there's nothing coming here with a mountainous home reputation. The O'Brien and Weld newcomers look OK, a little woolly in their coats, but fit enough. Instead, it's the Oxx debutant, Flying Plover, who looks the pick. She's not overly big, but her coat is good and there's a brightness to her that's appealing. Even desperation at this late stage isn't going to provoke a dash to the ring on the back of a hunch, but Flying Plover is 11–2 and maybe €50 on that pretty head mightn't be the dumbest thing. On balance, however, I decide it doesn't seem worth it.

Flying Plover finishes in the middle of the pack. Weld's horse wins – it's a good sign. The following race is the Group 3 Killavullan Stakes. Jupiter Pluvius is favourite and a confident nap in the paper on the back of reports that he's the main Guineas hope for Ballydoyle in 2008. Then word comes for Famous Name – apparently, he cut his leg early in the National Stakes and that run is best ignored. Sure enough, money starts to pour on the Weld runner. Even at 9–2, he's a perfectly reasonable bet to beat the favourite. No doubt, more hard-headed punters will dismiss the decision to not wade in as a woolly headed indulgence, but that's to ignore the conviction boost that comes from watching Jupiter Fluvius beat off Famous Name by three parts of a length. Now is the time to follow the fateful Plan.

Apparently, John Magnier's wife, Sue, is responsible for naming most of the Ballydoyle horses. She has come up with some inspired ones, like King Of Kings, and more grandiosely monickered animals that almost invariably end up running out of the money in deadend maidens. Compared to the legions of composers, dancers and statesmen that end up belting around gaff racetracks, she was clearly up all night coming up with a name for the son of Storm Cat and Spain. In fact, considering the sire is the world's dearest with a fee of $500,000, and the dam is a Breeders' Cup winner, Plan could feel more than a little peeved at carrying such a nondescript name – if you could picture him getting upset about anything.

Leopardstown's pre-parade ring is more bare now, with the oak trees shedding their leaves, and even fewer people leaning on the rails looking at the horses getting tacked up. Aidan O'Brien isn't here either. He's still in America after a disastrous Breeders' Cup that ended calamitously with George Washington breaking a leg and having to be put down in front of the Monmouth Park stands. Following days of torrential rain, the charismatic horse took his final steps on a dirt track that looked more like the Ypres salient than a racecourse. The whole meeting didn't look pretty, with almost every horse and jockey coming back looking as if they'd crossed no-man's land. The conditions provoked some rather hysterical reaction on this side of the pond, with quite a lot of hand-wringing from the same people who'll view the end of a four-mile slog in winter mud around Chepstow as a thing of beauty. Dirt racing is what it is, but if ever there has been an advertisement for synthetic surfaces, then Breeders' Cup 2007 takes some beating.

Such international thoughts don't really apply to the Irish Stallion Farms Maiden. Most of the eighteen runners are having their first sight of a racecourse and reactions are varied. One is getting noticeably colty, a neutral phrase that hardly does justice to the weaponry which the adolescent racehorse is unsheathing. Ballyvourney, on the other hand, is just being odd, fly-leaping and kicking out, with the sort of demented energy that those from the West Cork village he's named after would be proud of. In comparison, Plan is exhibiting all the laid-back calm that Mahler had here back in the spring. The difference is that Plan has already had a run. The regally bred colt with the dopey white nose was apprentice ridden when fifth at Cork. Today, he's got Heffernan on his back and with the ammunition available to O'Brien for a race like this, Plan's status as the stable choice looks significant. It becomes even more significant when there's a brief glimpse of 7–2 in the ring.

That doesn't last long. Almost immediately, the price drops to 3–1 and there's little percentage in waiting on the chance of it extending again. Up against Plan is an Oxx horse called Soul Murmur who ran third on his debut in a good maiden. However, he is by Indian Ridge whose stock usually relish soft ground. Also in the race is Sufad who looks great, and another one of those dangerous Weld newcomers called Winchester. Still, the hunch that put Plan in the morning double has turned into something approaching confidence.

Rarely has the value of a run been better illustrated. Plan jumps well and secures a perfect position behind his market rivals. Making the pace is an outsider who dutifully starts to come back to the field when they hit the straight. Heffernan eases out and Plan sprints away. The €900 to €300 is secure well before the line. The bonus is that there's the chance of a tasty bonus if Princess Rose Anne can bring off the double.

A shrewd move at this stage would be to lay off some of the bet. The filly is a hunch, based on her trainer's record in Nursery's and it's a wide open race too. However, once again, recklessness gets the better of calculation. Plan's win means it has been a good day anyway. If Princess Rose Anne loses, it won't be the end of the world. But she doesn't lose. It's desperately tight but, after being dashed from the stalls, there's enough left in the engine to just hold on in a tight finish. Proof, once again, that when your eye is in, it tends to pay off with a vengeance.

That mood continues to the Listed race where Laywaan is an interesting proposition of the sort that one examines only when well ahead of the game. Just one run this year means she's fresh, which is always a plus at this time of year, and the unlikely fast ground doesn't look ideal for a lot of the others. Once again, the value of checking them out in the parade ring pays off. Laywaan looks OK, but no more than that. There are plenty in the race who catch the eye more. It doesn't look worth it and, sure enough, she finishes well behind.

It means another one of those rare good days that end up provoking relief at getting it right and regret at not having more on. A pay-off of almost €2,200 nearly doubles the tally and it could hardly come at a better time. There are only two meetings left, back at Leopardstown next weekend. Even a mathematical moron can figure out that one make or break gamble can turn this whole season into an unlikely success. Put this overall profit on top of the original €5,000 tank and a 4–1 winner will damn near do the job. Play the profit alone and one 8–1 shot will all but bring up the total.

Maybe it's the feel-good factor from having won but, right now, it doesn't feel like mission impossible. After months of rare, unimaginable highs and a lot more bottom-of-the-barrel lows, there's actually a chance of bringing this off. It might mean a white-knuckle ride scary enough to put any roller-coaster into a scrapyard, but, still, there is an actual chance, and, at this stage, no one can ask for more. Plus, there's a horse due to run next Sunday that might, just might, be the one.

Running total: + €4,838

Beached on the Nile

4 November

In 2001, the then Finance Minister, Charlie McCreevy, introduced the Special Saving Incentive Account scheme whereby the government pledged to top up whatever anyone saved by a quarter. The only problem was that over 1 million people had to wait five years to get their cash. And when they did, it was taxed.

Details like that don't do morale any harm at all going into today. It's a long-shot but, considering the dark financial holes visited already, things really could be a lot worse. That €5,000 tank from the spring has all but doubled by winter – and its tax free, which beats the hell out of any SSIA. It's actually not too shabby when you look at it in percentage terms. Sad to say, though, that percentage arguments don't carry quite the same kudos as hitting the financial bull's eye – turning €5,000 into €50,000 sounds a damn sight sexier than explaining the minutiae of a 96 per cent return on an initial investment. But there's still one final chance to pull out that something extra special.

McCreevy, in fact, would probably love this opportunity. A keen punter anyway, nothing would prevent the former Min for Fin getting €10,000 on and airily dismissing the chances of doing his dough. When it comes to finance, some are blessed with balls of steel while the rest of us make do with the more disposable variety. A lot of that has to do with your financial resources in the first place, but there's also the question of temperament. During a long career in charge of Europe's most vibrant economy, McCreevy played with billions and never looked like he lost a night's sleep. However, the idea of putting the entire shooting match on a single bet has been enough to cause a lot of tossing and turning in a more impoverished household.

That horrendous start all the way back in April remains too vivid in my memory to even consider using the bank. Too much stress and anxiety has gone into protecting it to now casually hand it over on one final throw of the dice. For the sake of mental stability alone, the idea has been banished, which is quite a turn around considering that, just seven months ago, a mental tug of war went on to prevent a death-or-glory splurge. But a lot has happened since then, too much for my impulsive nature not to have been affected in some way.

It's a different story with the profit. Get an 8–1 winner on the last day and it's all over – and there's a horse that has been winking out from the entries all week who just happens to be trading between 10–1 and 12–1 for the November Handicap. It's one of those wide-open, two-mile puzzlers that contains any number of horses with a chance and has a habit of throwing up decent-priced winners. Funnier things have happened, like Gordy's Lucky Fifteens, for instance. Considering the odds he has beaten, today's assignment is a walk in the park. It's the question of what the legal profession's most flamboyantly successful punter would do in this situation that has kept the flames burning on a do-or-die toss up with the profit. But, boring as it may be, it isn't going to happen.

The work that has gone into securing this comparatively measly pot means throwing it away now feels like a betrayal – though of what is not so clear. It's not like the cash is in a box underneath the bed, no middle-of-the-night ceremonies worshipping the glory of easy money are taking place. In fact, it's precisely because getting it was so bloody difficult that there now exists a nagging sense of responsibility not to do something stupid. So the plan is this: Man On The Nile will carry €500 on his nose in the November Handicap and if by some miracle he wins, the whole lot of it will go on something in the very last race. That's the theory anyway – whether or not I've enough spine to do it is another matter. Man On The Nile should be a 10–1 chance, which means €5,500 going on to a shot in the dark. It's ridiculously optimistic but, at the same time, if it's going to happen, it's going to happen. All that's needed is for fate to be a lady one more time.

Already, though, there's a suspicion that a copout will be

found. After all, it's the simplest thing right now to find a horse in the last, stick it into a €500 double and let the wheel turn. That would be more like it – a bit like burning the boats and turning to face the enemy. It's a nice thought, but there's too long to ponder it in the days leading up to the meeting. All the 'what ifs' start queuing up. Like, what if taking tens about Man On The Nile means missing out on a bigger price if he drifts? Or, what if some late info comes along that the second leg isn't fancied at all and the whole kit-and-caboodle is already on? It would be disastrous, which is why this peep over the cliff at the burning boats below results in a less than heroic response.

Failing the punting challenge, however, isn't all that bad. It might seem hopelessly middle-aged to duck the big chance, but everyone's horizons are coloured by their circumstances. €5,000 wouldn't cost Messrs Magnier and McManus a thought. Apparently, they bet bigger on putts when they play golf together. Once, McManus even had to be reminded that a Cheltenham festival winner of his was even running in the race, but he still had €5,000 each way at 50–1 to pay, as he put it, 'for the party'. Still, there are many out there who would sell parts of their anatomy for the €500 I'm throwing at today's racing. Anyway, it's probably best not to think too deeply about the inequalities of the world when walking into a racetrack. After all, we're all guilty of something, it's only a tiny few who are as guilty as hell.

Virgil is here as well, checking out the possibility of one last touch before settling down to hibernate for the winter. Dundalk will keep the flat-racing flame flickering for another few weeks but old habits die hard and he is not alone in still treating November Handicap day as the last real kick of the season. 'A decent year,' is his verdict. 'It'll keep me going for the winter anyway!'

'Got anything for today?'

'I don't know. It's very difficult, with the ground so hard,' he replies. 'How about you?'

To his credit, he doesn't laugh out loud at the idea that two big-price winners might suddenly come up. In fact, he concedes that Man On The Nile has a chance. Then he flicks though his racecard. The Wachman filly will win the first, Virgil reckons, Observation Post will definitely win the Nursery and Orbit O'Gold has a big chance in the November. Flicking to the end of the card, he then jabs a finger at Grantsville in the last race. 'That has a chance. And it'll be a big price,' he says.

A glance at the paper says Grantsville could be as big as 12–1. It's perfect, if we can get to that stage with sufficient loot to invest in him and, for that to happen, we need Man On The Nile to win.

The shape of the big handicap is changed when one of the leading fancies, Al Eile, is pulled out along with two others. It means a reduction in everything's price, including Man On The Nile who's now trading at a general 7–1. That'll mean €4,000 going on to Grantsville – in theory. To be fair, it's not a complete fantasy – without wishing to come across all Doris Day about it, last Monday's acceptance that 'what will be, will be' continues to provide some comfort. There's no denying that Man On The Nile has a chance, and enough happens in the early races to emphasise that no amount of expertise is a guarantee of success.

Observation Post, for instance, starts a 9–4 favourite for the Nursery and is beaten after a furlong. He runs into early interference and then completely destroys his chance by refusing to settle. Gratitude that I chose to keep my powder dry until the big race intensifies even further after the Eyrefield Stakes, when Alessandro Volta chooses to break his maiden in a much better race than the one he got beat in at Navan three weeks ago.

He's barely past the post when the names of the runners for the November Handicap appear on the boards and a brief glimpse of 8–1 about Man On The Nile vanishes. That old tussle rears up between regret at missing the price and encouragement that he's clearly fancied by someone else. Not once is there a sign of any eights reappearing and, as the horses canter past on the way to the start, the final decision is taken: €3,500 to €500 it is. The cards are in the air. Only then does Chris Hayes' agent appear.

Since Hayes is riding Man On The Nile, the first question aimed at his pal is not about his take on the current state of Sino-Tibetan relations.

'He's fancied, right?' is my somewhat tremulous query.

'What is? Man On The Nile? Nah, a slow bastard: he's just the only one I could get him on. You haven't backed it, have you?'

'Just a little.'

If there's one thing a racecourse teaches, it is that a lot of what is said on it is horse manure. People talk for the sake of hearing their own voices, terrified that they may not appear to be in the know. Unfortunately, this guy does know what he's talking about.

Right from the start, Hayes never looks comfortable. He's on the rail and tailing the favourite but is simply not quick enough to keep his position. Entering the back straight, Man Of The Nile is being rowed along. At halfway, he gets a few sharp cracks of the whip. The response is plenty of effort but little speed. On the turn in, a brief hope of a staying on run through the pack is dashed with a piece of interference. Man Of The Nile keeps going and, at the line, he's a closest at finish sixth. And that's it. The show's over.

It's definitely an anti-climax. The faint hope of a grandstand finish has been keeping the dream machine ticking over for the last week. It hasn't felt completely unreasonable to believe the double could come off. For one thing, it would have fitted perfectly into the story, except that kind of perfect climax only happens in films that carry an 18 certificate. Reality, however, can rarely be choreographed, and racing reality never is. Despite everything, my overriding emotion is simple relief. Ending up just over, €4,000 ahead can't disguise one overwhelming reality – I'm a lousy punter. Not in the purely financial sense. In fact, add a zero to the original tank, and all the resultant bets, and this profit margin would allow a perfectly acceptable income. Except that would mean being a professional and being dependent on getting it right. My nerves are shot to hell as it is – even the idea of having a mortgage payment riding on the result of a seven-furlong handicap at Ballinrobe is causing facial tics. How the pros do it, and apparently enjoy doing it, remains a mystery. This whole project felt like too much of a duty far too often to allow even the faintest suspicion that another pro-punter is about to join the ranks.

Ultimately, it comes down to not needing to bet in order to enjoy a race. Without wishing to be all 'hooray Henry' and 'jolly hockey sticks' about it, there's enough drama going on out on the track anyway without having to have just that little bit more on than is affordable to get a buzz. That doesn't mean abstinence – there's nothing quite like backing your judgement and being proved right – but it's just too scary when you're depending on it.

That reality is emphasised in the very last race. Grantsville travels like a dream throughout. He makes ground around the final turn, gets a perfect split at the right time and bounds clear of the pack. The only problem is that Do The Trick has already done the same in front. If there had been €4,000 riding on it, Leopardstown's cleaners would have had an extra puddle to clear up. Maybe that kind of emotional roller-coaster is fun to some people but, for the rest of us, it's only torture.

An unexpected sideline of these months, however, has been on the tipping side. In fact, following my own advice might have helped things along considerably. There have been days, apparently, when the stuff in the paper has actually read like it has been written by someone who knows what he's on about. Phrases like 'value' and 'too short a price' have been cropping up enough to have impressed Gordy and both other readers: which only goes to prove that some of us have more luck than we deserve.

There have been blindspots, however. Apparently, Regalline's name has also kept cropping up in tips, which is unfair considering not a cent more went on her after Day One. Maybe it was sentiment that encouraged desire for all that morning speed to eventually last out until the afternoon. But it didn't. The great hope ran nine times and only finally won a race at Listowel in September. Enough people kept the faith to make her favourite and she scraped home, winning, as the *Racing Post* put it, by a very short head. Right now, she's at stud, enjoying her happy fate, free of the requirement to run very fast with a little man on her back.

She's a sobering reminder of how fickle this racing game is, and she's a reminder that everyone will very quickly forget. That's because there is always a new 'fucking machine' just waiting to go. It's what the whole sport, industry, business – whatever you want to call it – is based on. The most cynical stroke trainer will always welcome a new horse into the yard with the hope that this will be the champion of a lifetime. Even hard-headed punters will succumb to the enticement of an unraced two-year-old that might just be the next big thing. The dream is the thing, and there will always be a dream because there will always be the next race.

That's why there's at least one bruised, exhausted, but relieved fan leaving Leopardstown with a greater love for the game than ever before. Even now, facing into a long winter, there's a name rattling around my noggin that will keep a little glow of anticipation going until the New Year. He's an unraced three-year-old, trained on the Curragh and is owned by a sheikh. Apparently, he really is a machine. He's bay, he's brilliant, and his name is D—.

Come on now, nothing's completely free in this world. You'll just have to wait until I'm on first!

Final total: + €4,338

Just Think Gandhi

5 November

Often at the end of 'how to' books, there's a list of dos and don'ts. After presenting abundant evidence of 'how not to' do something, it might seem like serious chutzpah to try that here. However, since waiting for credibility in the betting game could entail waiting forever, let's just do it anyway. Listed below are ten tips for not going completely broke. It's a purely personal list, of course, and doesn't contain what might be the most valuable tip of all which is to ignore any newspaper hack's recommendations on anything. But if it's hardly a plan to live life by, it's at least presented in weary good faith after months of staring down the betting barrel.

1. Ditch the family. The warm bosom of a busy and satisfying domestic existence is invaluable in everything else, but it's a disaster for anyone with delusions of making a living from punting. Travel, work and almost twenty-four-hour domination of the television are not compatible with two boisterous boys and a better half devoted to reality TV. Arguing that watching every race, the lead up to it, and a couple of replays, is vital for Daddy to take everyone to Mauritius for the winter eventually wears thin. Mild beatings can get the kids out of the way for a while. However, arguing that *Big Brother* is a vapid insult to human intelligence isn't really a shrewd move against a woman who can be fascinated by the gobby bird on *BB* while, at the same time, arguing how Klimt's landscapes are, in fact, much better than the nudey stuff. Not being in charge of the remote control doesn't hurt half as much as being intellectually horse-whipped by your significant other – unless you're into it.

2. Go racing. Unless you're luckier than God, there's little or no way to make betting pay in Ireland unless you are a regular racegoer. And by regular, we're talking three or four days a week during the summer. That requires either a flow of outside money that makes betting pretty much irrelevant, or else you do it full-time in an attempt to gain that exalted status. It is remarkable how much can be picked up just by being at the track, perhaps not in the sense of a 'smoking gun' nugget of information, but just in the general ebb and flow of

racecourse gossip. Quite a strong filter is required to distil the good stuff from the bad but it is remarkable how quickly such a sensibility develops when there's enough money depending on it. It's also important to see the horses in the paddock. There are plenty of people who are willing to clothe the process of distinguishing a fit, healthy horse from its opposite in a fog of jargon, but it basically comes down to being thin, shiny and healthy. Just think Gandhi.

3. Realise that 99 per cent of what you hear on a racecourse is Grade A crap. This may seem to contradict tip No. 2, but a cheery belief in the goodness of your fellow man is not a sound business plan when it comes to gambling. Mostly, it isn't malicious crap, just people sounding off for the sake of wanting to appear like they know what they're talking about. Occasionally, however, everyone gets, to use the phrase, 'put away', by one of life's perverts who believes in getting his retaliation in first. Perverts aside, it is important to tap into the crap current too – knowing what isn't fancied can often be just as important as knowing what is.

4. Learn to read between the lines. Trainers and jockeys are creatures of habit, the same as the rest of us, and it doesn't take long before certain patterns start to develop. To everyone else, your pretty patterns might seem the result of too many hallucinogenic drugs, but learn to trust them. For instance, Aidan O'Brien has a habit of throwing some two-year-old first-timers

straight into Listed or Group race company and often they run very well. However, treating that as an indication that they are at the top of the pecking order in Ballydoyle can be dangerous. Great Barrier Reef, runner up in the Gimcrack at York in August, is a good example. Those betting on normal improvement from that got their fingers burned a number of times. The real O'Brien top-notchers go the traditional route and kick off in maidens.

5.   Bet each way. There's no point fighting it. Yes, it's double the stake but, depending on the size of the race, it can mean up to four more chances to finish ahead. The bookies will say each way in handicaps is how they lose, but it's 3–1 and better each way in maidens that can be the real pay-off. On decent ground, there are twenty-five runner maidens being run where, most of the time, only about four or five of the horses can possibly win. Betting each way in these races is the real shrewdie play, betting each way doubles every day for weeks on end is not.

6.   Read everything. Contrary to the widespread impression that newspaper hacks go out of their way to persecute the innocent, harass the famous, and accelerate the dumbing down process, most scribblers go about their business in as professional a manner as they can manage. The stuff might not always be right, but there is no grand 'meeeja' plan to con everyone. In fact, the reality is that punters have never had it so good in terms

of information. Compared to many major racing countries, coverage in the national dailies in Ireland and the UK is of a quantity and standard that many other sports can only envy. Throw in the trade papers, plus the enormous resources available on the web, and punters have a good thing going.

7. Get the best technology. There are few things more maddening than dealing with bog-standard internet access. That green line slowly inching its way across the bottom of the screen will, eventually, put you in a bed next to a much larger screen with lots more green lines measuring your heart rate. Suck it up and pay for the best possible broadband, although, in Ireland, that might only delay any hospital visit.

8. Specialise. With the amount of racing that's now going on all through the year, it's becoming increasingly difficult to keep a calculating eye on all the form. So it makes sense to concentrate on certain areas. Sprint handicaps, for instance, are a minefield for most of us, but there are people out there who swear by them. Likewise, there are others who do nothing but bet on two-year races. The introduction of all-weather racing in Dundalk opens up a brand-new betting avenue. Turf form will clearly still play a large part in analysing runners, but proven ability on the synthetic surface has to count for a lot.

9. Don't ride the emotional rails. Getting over-excited after a win will only make failures feel even worse. That doesn't mean turning into some cold, calculating creature of habit; it simply means keeping things in perspective.

10. ENJOY IT. The most important of all. Anyone already hoovering half of Colombia up their nose, or depositing a couple of bottles of whiskey a day into a hollow leg, might not be best advised to find out for themselves how enjoyable betting on the horses can be. But, compulsives apart, there are few more fun things to do than backing yourself to win, because, basically, that is what every bet is. It doesn't matter what you bet on: it's your judgement that's at stake as much as your money and we all need to be right sometimes. In fact, get it right 51 per cent of the time, and you'll turn into a bit of a betting hero – and there are never enough heroes in the world.

Aw, Crap

6 November

Mahler finishes third in Australia's most famous race, the Melbourne Cup. This absence of an each way gene is a killer.

Acknowledgements

There wouldn't be a book without Niamh so, if you don't like it, blame her.

Very special thanks to my mum and dad, and everyone in the O'Connor tribe.

A big thank you to Jonathan Williams whose patience and unfailing support has been hugely important.

Claire, Ciara and everyone at Hachette Books Ireland who have taken a gamble of their own on this. Let's hope they collect on all their hard work.

I'm indebted to a number of people who would rather remain unnamed but whose help is very much appreciated.

Thanks to *The Irish Times* for the gig.

And then there's Peter and Johnny, who just happen to mean everything.